Trading in the Zone

Maximizing Performance with Focus and Discipline

ARI KIEV

John Wiley & Sons, Inc

New York • Chichester • Weinheim • Brisbane • Singapore • Toronto

Library of Congress Cataloging-in-Publication Data:

Kiev, Ari.
    Trading in the zone : maximizing performance with focus and discipline /
Ari Kiev.
        p. cm.
    Expanded version of: Trading to win, c1998.
    ISBN 0-471-37908-5 (cloth : alk. paper)
    1. Electronic trading of securities. 2. Investments. 3. Stock exchanges.
    4. Investment analysis. I. Kiev, Ari. Trading to win. II. Title.
HG4521.K455   2001
332.63′2′02854678—dc21

                                                                        00-050456

Printed in the United States of America

10 9 8 7 6 5 4 3 2 1

For my wife, Phyllis,
with love and appreciation.

Acknowledgments

As with my previous book, *Trading to Win*, many people have helped me to understand the complexities of trading.

First and foremost, I want to thank the various firms with which I have worked and that have provided me the opportunity to assist traders to tap their hidden potential and produce extraordinary results in the high stress environment of trading.

I am grateful to the various traders with whom I have worked who have provided the impetus to dig deeper into the arcane byways of the trading art, and to those who read and commented on portions of the manuscript and helped me to clarify some of the concepts I have examined in this book.

Finally, I want to thank Tricia Brown for her yeoman's work throughout the entire development and writing of this book from start to finish and Grace Lichtenstein who so kindly reviewed the book in its last stages.

And of course, this could not have been accomplished without the unceasing support and encouragement of my wonderful wife, Phyllis, who has once again helped me to realize my dreams.

A. K.

Contents

Introduction   **1**

Part One   Getting in the Zone

Chapter 1   Defining the Zone   **11**

How to Enter the Zone   14

How to Be in the Zone   16

How to Stay in the Zone   18

Chapter 2   Overcoming the Past   **21**

Identifying Past Programming   22

Modifying Your Behavior   28

Chapter 3   Using a Goal   **33**

Setting the Goal   34

Resisting the Goal-Setting Approach   38

Implementing a Strategy   41

Maintaining the Mental Groove   45

Staying Committed   48

Part Two   Preparing for the Trade

Chapter 4   Gathering Information   **53**

The Need for Good Analysis   54

Determining What Is Pertinent   56

Processing the Information   60

Timing Is Important   65

Chapter 5   Understanding the Analysis   **69**
Using Technical Analysis   70
Examining Technical Indicators   71
Understanding Macro   74

Chapter 6   Learning More   **81**
Gaining an Edge   82
Finding Value in a Company   83
Fundamental Reasons to Buy   87
Understanding the Unseen Variables   92

Part Three   Controlling the Risk

Chapter 7   Managing the Risk   **99**
Review Your Statistics   101
Play Bigger   108
Building a Portfolio   112

Chapter 8   Tolerating the Pain   **117**
Control Your Emotions   118
Handle the Losses   126

Part Four   Trading Consistently

Chapter 9   Learning from Your Mistakes   **135**
Picking Tops or Bottoms   136
Holding on to Losers   138
Failing to Take Profits   144
Bidding for Stocks   147
Relying on Intuition   148
Overtrading   149
Reviewing Mistakes   150

Chapter 10   Overcoming Psychological Obstacles   **157**
Letting Go of Seller's Remorse   159
Perfectionism and Paralysis   161
The "Poor Me" Syndrome   166
Combating Complacency   169
Inability to Adjust   170
Clearing the Hurdles   174

Chapter 11 Stepping Up to the Challenge **175**
Continue the Challenge   176
Do Practice Visual Imagery Rehearsal   178
Do Go Further   180
Do Focus   183
Don't Abandon Your Opinion   186
Don't Say "Burnt Out"   187
Don't Withdraw   188
Take the Step   190

Part Five   Using Advanced Strategies

Chapter 12 Taking Advantage of Capitulation **195**
Defining Capitulation   196
Trading in a Collapsing Market   199
Managing in Inflection   201

Chapter 13 Short Selling **205**
Developing a Thesis   206
Defining a Good Short   208
Perfecting the Timing and Relevance   212
Managing the Psychology   215

Conclusion **219**

Index **227**

Introduction

Thomas Edison performed 2,999 experiments before he invented the electric light bulb—a fact reflective of his incredible perseverance in the face of defeat. Edison's experience is an inspirational model for people from all walks of life but especially for traders who must learn to remain committed to their objectives in spite of repeated failures.

While a few traders are so-called naturals and from the start seem to thrive in the emotionally charged, high-risk activity of trading, most traders must work at learning psychologically sound ways of riding out the highs and lows and especially at learning how to persevere in the face of failure. My first trading book, *Trading to Win*, focuses on psychological strategies for successful trading. *Trading in the Zone* expands on these themes and represents three more years of experience in working with a variety of traders on issues ranging from portfolio size and strategy to traditional coaching issues pertaining to performance, motivation, and recovery from failure.

Having helped a number of traders to perform exceedingly well, I wanted to dig deeper in terms of finding additional ways to help traders achieve even greater levels of excellence. Through the use of risk management statistics, I was able to speed the process of identifying trading behaviors that needed tweaking or modification. By reviewing and

1

recreating the positive mind-set of past positive trades on a daily basis, I was able to help other traders bolster their confidence in selecting and staying with specific trades and to mentally and emotionally enter the zone before the day started.

Although the basic principles of *Trading to Win* continue to influence my work with traders, in this book I also focus on ways of staying in the "zone"—that combination of positive mind-set, focused attention, and adherence to trading discipline that allows the best traders to keep on producing outstanding results day after day, year after year.

Over time it soon became apparent that the same principles outlined in *Trading to Win* could be applied to digging deeper for information, because it is the tradability of particular ideas that is important, not just understanding the company. By understanding the subtleties of price action, the nature of the market, macroeconomic factors, and the like, traders could be assisted in making the right choices.

As one fast-rising trader told me, "You can't rest on your laurels. Yesterday doesn't give me anything for today. The zone psychologically prepares you to focus. I have the ideas and know-how to do it. For me it is all psychological. It is execution and being focused. Following the discipline helps me to get into the zone. The zone is where you are disciplined and centered, and the trade is working. Once you have the judgment, research, and ideas, it is just confidence and risk-taking. The mental rehearsal gives me more confidence."

Most traders believe that "getting into the zone" happens when you have "a hot streak." I believe you can create the zone. The zone is a psychological state. It is when you are focused, disciplined, and fully engaged in the process at hand. Being "in the zone" doesn't necessarily mean winning. However, trading in the zone will certainly increase your capacity to perform and succeed.

Ultimately, being in the zone is about self-control and focus, the ability to recover and sustain momentum. It means doing all the things you have trained to do so that regardless of your results, you can begin the next day with the same degree of energy and enthusiasm that you had today. Learning to trade in the zone is about shifting your frame of reference, defining a far-reaching objective, and then filling in the pieces in terms of what the objective requires.

Trading is a complicated process due to the emotions triggered by the incredible volatility and unpredictability of the market and the roller-coaster ups and downs that are daily experienced by traders. There are emotional waves activated by wide swings of success and failure and by the impact these responses have on the way you continue to trade. It is easy to try to find ways of reducing the anxiety and even reducing the euphoria by disengaging from the process.

For the past eight years I have been working with top-notch Wall Street traders unearthing specific psychological issues that interfere with the trading process. These include resistance, fear of failure, defensive behavior, negative self-characterizations, and negative mind-sets that become self-fulfilling prophecies.

It is important to see how these issues keep you from using your talents, distract you from your strategy, and get you to trade too many stocks and sectors. Anxiety may lead to poor selections, picking hot names rather than good names, and hesitating and holding back.

For example, inexperienced traders may get attached to their own ideas or to stocks. They may get out of winning trades to get a quick profit, hold on to losing trades, and lose more money in losing trades than they make in winning trades. When a trade goes against them, it may set off a losing cycle where they can't separate from the trade, clear their thinking, and get back into the flow. This anxiety exacerbates the cycle and leads to more of the same errors. Anxiety leads to a tendency to hold while a stock drops until the trader is devastated and loses confidence. Better traders admit they are confused, fearful, or don't know. They ask for help or reduce the size of their positions until they are in the right mind-set to start winning. They realize the self-fulfilling prophecy that a losing mind-set creates.

To be most successful, traders must recognize the repetitive patterns in their behavior and the situations where there are opportunities to extend themselves, to extend their horizons, or to change their perspectives. Once a trader is out of the negative mind-set, he or she is better able to use information as well as to enter into the zone.

The best traders don't get attached to their stocks. They recognize that there are forces they cannot understand. Like Zen masters, they are able to be in the now and evaluate where they ought to be on

RESILIANCE

LET IT FLOW LET IT GO

the basis of where the stock is and where it is going. They don't let their own good or bad feelings or hopes or beliefs color their choices or decisions. They take a loss, clear their heads, center, and focus, and don't try to make it back in that same stock. They continually read the market rather than allowing feelings about the stocks to impinge on their trading. Traders need to contain those natural distortions that interfere with their capacity to see the reality of the market or the tape.

You need to develop a discipline based on understanding the way you personally are trading and playing the game. To trade in the zone, you need to learn the application of intelligence, communication skills, reading, and taking notes on what you are doing. Keep track of your scores, your trades, and ways of improving the elements of your game. The results will multiply dramatically. Face the truth and be honest with yourself. Recognize where you did stupid things or believed too much in your own ability. Recognize when you are not looking objectively at what you are doing.

STRATEGIES

Play your winning names. Stay with what has been working in the event you want to double up. Avoid stocks that don't move. Make rules that are personal and related to your trading style. Adherence to them will improve the quality of your game. Find a coach, a partner, or someone you trust who will keep you honest and on your game. Consider trading with a team whose joint profit and loss (P&L) can have value in providing a cushion and allowing you to trade bigger-sized positions, with the confidence that the group is behind you. Share fears, doubts, and mistakes so you don't spend too much energy covering them up. Get support from others. You need to be able to share your concerns and ask for help.

KEY, SWING, THOUGHT, FOCUS

Most of this book is based on intensive training sessions with traders where I have focused on trading styles, trading problems, the psychological states to enter into to maximize trading, diversifying risk in personnel, and developing the profitability of selected traders on the team. This book represents an expansion of *Trading to Win* and explores more strategies for winning, more negative trading loops, and more applications to other trading instruments. It also examines more approaches to mastering the self through observation, review of the past, and modifying trading behavior to strengthen performance. The focus is on helping traders to do what they think they cannot and to discover new things about their trading.

Trading in the Zone can be read as a sequel to *Trading to Win* or on its own. Although I have sought to further develop some of the principles outlined in my previous book, I have also taken this opportunity to:

- Add a longer-term view to the trading strategies discussed.
- Examine more mistakes that traders can make.
- Review basic trading strategies and examine more complex strategies.
- Demonstrate additional ways to increase a trader's psychological edge.

This book has been written not only to assist the professional trader but also the ordinary amateur trader and day trader as well. Taking into account the increasing use of the Internet for trading, the applications in this book can be of assistance to the home trader who trades once or twice a week as well as the career trader doing it every day.

The relative ease of entry into day trading through Internet access to online brokerages, the easy access to stock market information, and the continuation of the biggest and longest bull market in history have set the stage for a lot of amateurs to get into trading. Amateur traders may get hooked on trading because of a few quick and easy wins, much as people get hooked on gambling. Random wins and losses create an inconsistent pattern of reinforcement that is habit forming. They then begin to focus attention on finding winning stocks rather than on learning the process. They are also likely to eventually lose because they become anxious and unable to behave as flexibly as the successful trader.

If you are a beginner, you need to get into the game by studying what you know and then systematically learning how to trade with fundamental information. Read information on the Internet. Find a mentor. Work as an assistant to a trader. Paper trade. Take courses. Know how to handle risk, loss, and stress. These activities are all parts of the trading experience.

In my work with professional traders, I have consistently found that the most successful make most of their profit from 3 percent to 10 percent of their trades. Therefore, most of their trades are *not* making profit. Success is not about picking the right stocks. It is really about how well you do once you are in the trade. Good traders stay with winning trades. They keep adding to those positions. If one goes bad, they get out fast.

[handwritten margin note: MOST BETS DON'T]

I am often asked how, as a psychiatrist, I became interested in the psychology of trading. The answer is simple. Psychology, along with trading techniques and money management, is one of the foundations of successful trading because of the emotional and stressful nature of trading itself. Even experienced traders find that their emotional responses can get in the way and interfere with implementation of their money management skills and strategies. My work with traders has focused on these issues.

For example, one trader, Dylan, bought 2,500 shares of a telecom stock and made $15,000. If he had bought 7,500 shares he would have made more, but he wasn't that sure of the stock. I questioned whether he needed to do more work to increase his conviction and to trade at the level he wanted to trade. He was governed by his fear, held back, and hesitated to do what he needed. He was taking a chance instead of doing the work.

Therefore, my objective is to assist traders to change their behavior so as to increase their profitability. Part of this process is urging traders to be more analytical about themselves and what they are doing. Encouraging traders to participate in the process of discussion often requires cajoling, humor, and emotionality. I must get them to see how stuck they are in their mental and physical positions, encourage them to take bigger risks, and to think the impossible.

I am fundamentally concerned with helping traders to focus on ways of getting out of losing positions and expanding winning ones. As I see it, my principal function is to help teach traders to:

- Make decisions based on data-clear thinking.
- Define entry and exit points.
- Know when to get bigger.

[handwritten note at bottom: " GOVERNED BY YOUR FEAR?"]

- Handle uncertainty and cope with emotional responses.
- Avoid trying to win back losses.
- Sustain momentum.
- Recover from breakdowns and break through barriers.

Real profitability comes from maximizing the profit in good trades, which requires preparation and visualization of anticipated moves that will be made in response to events.

The critical function of this book is to teach you how to consciously define a target and then trade in terms of it. By making a conscious commitment and then measuring your performance and tracking your behavior, you can be more in the game.

Most trading overemphasizes current positions. The master trader has a longer-term focus, a goal, and a strategy to reach that goal. Because of this, he or she is able to tolerate the pain of losing. This ability requires learning the meaning of trading with no ego—letting the trade happen and getting out of the way.

It takes time to "reframe" the thinking of the trader so that he is willing to commit to a trading target beyond his current capability or his past performance. It is not simply a matter of following a formula. The process requires engaging him in a dialogue where he is willing (sometimes in the presence of his peers) to verbalize his expanded goal and face his fear of being ridiculed by the group. He must admit to the trading errors he has made that day and face the shame in the presence of others (including perhaps his boss). This process is softened by having others, including his boss, also admit to mistakes and old habits that were difficult to break.

In my work with traders I have learned to discover who a person is and what she needs to work on in her personality by watching her trade or listening to her report of her trading. I am always looking for the point of vulnerability or the stopping point where the most change can occur—the point where the trader stops out of fear or habit and where she has the chance, if shown, to enter into the arena of uncertainty and can trade past her own expectations.

By understanding your emotions, how you approach and enact a trade, and what your thinking is, I can help you achieve your objectives.

I will not tell you how or what to trade; I will teach you to understand your own anxiety and emotional responses to fluctuations in the market. I am not as concerned with your results as I am with helping you define a strategy consistent with your goal. When you develop such a goal-directed strategy, you will discover you can set and reach bigger objectives.

As one trader expressed it, "There is no better job in the world. I would take this over pro basketball, but you are your own enemy. You are the biggest obstacle to your success. You have to keep working on yourself all the time because your own psychology is ultimately the most limiting factor in the arena of trading." *Getting in your own way.*

In order to teach you how to trade in the zone, I have used many examples of the right and wrong ways of handling certain situations. However, the names of traders and the companies traded have been disguised. My intention is not to explicitly comment about particular individuals or companies, but to help you see the necessity of examining your trades to see what works and what doesn't and to determine what you need to do to stay on target. This book is about raising levels of *awareness* consciousness and developing the appropriate skills so that you, too, can trade in the zone.

Part One

Getting in the Zone

Chapter 1

Defining the Zone

Imagine a morning when almost as soon as you awake you eagerly anticipate heading for your office for a breakthrough day of trading. Even as you brush your teeth, your mind turns toward certain stocks and strategies. You are not overly anxious, but you feel more alert, more alive than usual.

Once you are at your desk, looking at your terminals, you feel as though you are really seeing the larger universe of the stock market as a whole, not as bits and pieces of data. You are clear-eyed and calm as you phone your contacts, scroll through numbers, glance at the Internet. Yet there is a special conviction to your moves. As you see opportunities, you place your orders one after the other, nimbly, as if you were a great quarterback effortlessly throwing pinpoint passes downfield.

You may be doing many things at once—multitasking on your computers, absorbing new numbers, chatting on the phone—yet you feel you are in control of each step you take. The tape is giving you positive feedback and your numbers are climbing, but you don't feel overly excited. You just keep going. Time passes without your being very conscious of it. You know you are pushing yourself to new heights, and it feels good. Welcome to the zone—a place all traders want to be, but most can't seem to find. In this chapter, I show you why you want to be in the zone, how to get there, and how to stay there.

The zone is an ideal psychological state where you are doing everything correctly. Your trades are working and there is no resistance. Entering the zone means allowing yourself to get into a centered state of mind and activating positive memories by remembering the sights, sounds, and smells of past positive experiences. With practice, most people can learn to tap into the power of these experiences so they can function beyond the constraints of limiting thoughts.

The zone allows you to trade in a disciplined way and yet be more open to opportunities. By being in the zone you can do more work with less effort and overcome inertia. Somewhere in the process, a "light" will go off and you will break through an internal barrier to expand your limits.

People who participate in high-risk sports can relate to being in the zone. They often get a sense of freedom, excitement, alertness, and the ability to focus with clarity while keeping panic at bay. Traders can feel this same sort of exuberance.

It is easier to remain in the zone when you are successful. It is far more difficult to sustain the zone when you are losing. The experience of loss is likely to activate earlier-learned defensive habits that act as constraints or inhibitions on your freedom to be creative. All of these thoughts are likely to intensify if you are unable to ask for or accept support from others.

Although you may be bothered by these thoughts and may be focusing your energy on trying to control them, your task really is to see them as part of a larger concept that is the overarching perspective through which you experience your life. Once you begin to realize what your typical conceptual limitations are, you will begin to see what can be changed in order to bring more power and forcefulness to your trading.

For example, your statements create the structure of thinking that you bring to your trading. As you become aware of your automatic thoughts, superstitions, beliefs, and the fixed ways you have of perceiving the world, you will begin to see how much of your thinking keeps reproducing the past and affects the results you produce.

Once you recognize these repetitive thoughts and can allow them to pass, you can redefine your trading objectives. Once you commit to concrete results, you can introduce extraordinary energy into your trading and begin to move toward recapturing the power of the zone. If, instead of these limiting notions of the past, you commit to a larger vision of the future as the guiding principle of your trading, you can begin to tap hidden dimensions in yourself and produce amazing results.

GOING FOR DREAMS RELEASED TALENT

Case Study
One trader, Timothy, found himself caught up in the emotion of having a good month. He almost backed out of a position because the market looked like it was turning, but then he realized that he was not trading according to his plan.

"I was trying to be judicious about kicking out some bad trades as opposed to holding them until the noise passed," he said. "I knew why I was in this trade. I had clearly defined the downside. I decided to stay in the trade."

Timothy caught himself trying to scalp out of a position because of anxiety and then decided to let the larger goal help him ride out his emotions. His goal became the lever for change.

"I identified the discomfort and didn't let it govern me," he continued. "I wanted to make an impression, have a positive month, solidify my P&L [profit and loss], not run any more risk as opposed to playing the game."

Trading in the zone is not impossible. Staying in the zone is difficult but still not impossible. It requires work, which begins by learning a set of skills. It is not something you accomplish on your own. If you are not in the zone, you need to consider that somewhere in the game you are holding back. You are not playing your best. Something is interfering with your performance.

One trader, Wayne, compares trading in the zone to driving in the rain: "The zone means to move as fast as you can while staying in control, because if you go one mile too fast you crash. Stay at the level you are comfortable, not going faster than you can control. To do this requires depth, knowledge, being able to explain what you are doing, understanding the mechanics of the business. The better fundamentals you have, the better you can perform, even when you do not have a good day."

He outlines four steps for reaching the zone:

1. Learn how to sell so that you don't get out too soon or too late.
2. Learn how to hold longer when you're winning.
3. Get more knowledge about companies and catalysts.
4. Take it from a "me" to an "us" group.

SELF 1 (EGO)

"If you are surrounded by players," he said, "then the team hums. I don't always have to score. You have to give up your ego. Think of what you can do as part of a process. Don't be bigger than the market. You don't master the ocean. You learn to live with it. You understand which way the winds are blowing and go with the flow. When you find the flows, you know when to stay out as well. I get in the zone through hard work." *COMMIT FOCUS WORK*

"Sometimes you are in the zone, and it feels natural. Sometimes when you are trading, you see the field more clearly. Most of the time you are fighting for information. It is not serendipity. I call friends. I call Tokyo. I get on the Internet. I have a group calling me. At some point the information clicks in, and you start to see things. You see the playing field, and you play as hard as you can." *GET IN ZONE BY GETTING INTO WHAT YOURE DOING.*

How to Enter the Zone

Players who are willing to get into the zone are willing to do the uncomfortable thing. They are willing to get bigger in the face of success, when everything within them is pushing them to take their profits or get smaller. This was well stated by Dennis, an experienced macro trader, who noted: "When I find an easy trade, it is usually wrong. In my bets, I am always so nervous that I never do enough. But when I am in the zone, I know I am nervous, but I put on huge positions. I did this in the Australian 10-year bond," he continued. "I traded against my own view because I saw a specific rare technical indicator, the so-called abandoned baby or doji chart pattern. It is the abandoned baby top where the market rallies and the next day everyone needs to buy. This is a blowoff as well. They all buy at the high. The next day it gaps lower, leaving the previous day's uptick alone or abandoned and unconnected to the next day's opening. This pattern gave me such comfort that I could trade it even though it was against my view. I knew this pattern was a rarity and, while I felt uncomfortable, this chart pattern gave me supreme confidence."

Even if you are playing at an advanced level, it is critical to assess the nature of your portfolio so that you begin to line up your trades in terms of a strategy that has been designed with your target in mind. Of course, you consider the necessary risk parameters that are critical for your firm.

Case Study

Let's look at the situation of Floyd, manager of a large portfolio of cyclical stocks. My discussions with him centered on the critical issue of establishing a $5 million per month portfolio. Floyd needed to see the necessity of getting bigger in certain positions if he were going to produce the result he wanted. His natural inclination, however, was to hold on to things he liked, even if they didn't meet his criteria. He also tried to get out of or minimize strong positions because he already had "sufficient amounts" of stock in them.

Getting into the zone for this trader meant looking at his risk/reward profile and his conviction of certain trades, and a redistribution of his trades so that he was putting more of his capital to work on the stocks in which he had higher conviction. This redistribution was not as easy to do as one might think. He had set up his portfolio to be balanced rather than to be optimal. To get into the zone, to play to win, for him meant to realign his portfolio so that it was designed for success without putting him in any greater risk. This approach meant putting more money into better trades where he had more conviction, adding to these positions from positions where he had less conviction, trading on a daily basis to make shorter-term profits in longer-term positions, and taking advantage of intraday volatility. Therefore, when a stock had moved as far as it could go in a given day—say two or three points—and there were other stocks that were shorter term but were beginning to move, he had to have the courage to take his profit from the longer-term trade and put his capital to better usage in the shorter-term trade. Next, he had to take the profit from that and put it in other good short-term trades. This nimbleness required paying attention to more variables, but it began to increase his daily profitability and enabled him to get closer to his monthly target.

Of course, getting in the zone means different things for different *people* traders. For Raymond, it meant getting back in touch with his willingness to take risk and to get support from his team. Raymond had to be ready to give up his individualistic self-sufficient approach and embrace the support of others who could help him get past his fears and inhibitions. He had to get past his fearful state of paralysis and move toward his vision, taking the risk associated with trading at those levels without being afraid of the consequences.

Entering the zone requires conviction. Conviction comes from a willingness to trade your ideas and to develop confidence in your ability to assess what moves to make. Some traders erroneously think that conviction comes from more certainty or from feeling positive. I tell them that when Shaquille O'Neal is off in his shooting, he keeps shooting until he gets back into the groove. Traders have to keep trading until they find the zone. It will not appear by itself. It will appear only from the effort made to keep moving until they get a feel for the market and for the right trades. Jordan, an experienced trader, communicated this thought: "The ability to trust my feelings is the key to it. I will keep trading some positions until I get them right. Finally, I have the confidence to stick with my convictions. When I think I am right, I will stay there. I don't care how the stock trades." *TRUST VOICE NO RESISTANCE*

How to Be in the Zone

HYPO FRONTALITY / No SELF / Peak attention
How do you know that you are in the zone? You know you are there when you are totally focused. Time stands still. You hit the ball effortlessly with no resistance. It's like taking an exam. When you know the answers, they jump out of the questions. *NO JUDGMENT*

You know you are in the zone when you see things you have prepared to see. There is less resistance, and it feels good. Time slows, extends itself. You feel at one with the game. To get there requires focusing and tuning out other things. You cannot be bothered by ordinary concerns.   *PARK ATTENTION*

PROCESS OVER RESULTS

Being in the zone means staying on target. Success is secondary. The zone is "getting high from finding a great idea, which may take months of work to actually find," said Phillip.

Another trader described it this way: "There's a spot where I don't get caught up in the marketing muck. I can still float in and catch the big trades and not get back in between. As you are up big and your goal is in sight, you feel less pressure that the daily numbers have to be there, and the numbers just flow in."   *LET Allow*

Being in the zone means following your strategy, trusting your plan. Jordan is a good trader. His percentage of winning trades is almost 70 percent. He is confident in his abilities. "I stay in things until I am right," he said. "I did the work. If I thought I was right, I didn't care how they traded. I stayed with them. I am trading bigger. The ability to trust my feelings is the key. Other traders may say that they should buy something but then they don't. Some have incredible analyses, but they just won't act."

When you are in the zone you are trading with a lack of concern for results. You are trading according to a plan, and you have a greater tolerance for pain. However, you cannot let this tolerance push you out of control.

If you ski, your natural tendency is to try to control the skiing, but then you fall. Skiing is learning to control the slide. With more maneuverability, you can allow for more free fall. Gravity and sliding take over when you quit holding on so tightly. You may fall, but you also experience more exhilaration.

For example, let's say a trade is going well. Something that was going down is now moving up. However, instead of moving with that, getting more information, and getting bigger, you get scared and take your profits and run. The better traders, however, trust their instincts, take the risk, and stay in the game longer.   *LET GO*

That capacity to trust your instinct and go with the flow is where you are allowing yourself to experience the phenomenon of trading in the zone. It is like the sweet spot in tennis when you just focus on the ball. You don't watch the stands or think about the last shot. Your mind is clear, and you focus on what is in front of you—a biomechanically perfect swing. When you are free of extraneous thoughts, free of self-criticism, replaying past disasters or fearful thoughts, you can become centered and focused.   *STRIP YOUR SCRIPT   RIP NEW SCRIPT*

To be in the zone means that you are using your goal as a lens through which to see the actions you need to take. If you find yourself making trades that are ultimately not in your own best interest, step back and look at what you are doing.

"Everyone trades differently," said Wayne. "The key is to understand your own risk profile. One trader I know, for example, is comfortable losing $200,000 on a trade. After that, he'll bail out. I don't have the loss appetite. How much can you tolerate? Is it 1,000 shares down a point or 1,000 shares down half a point? Your risk appetite should be clearly defined. You need to feel you are in control but still have enough room that you can be right or wrong and not get stopped out."

Among highly trained athletes with appropriate mechanics, there are still factors that differentiate the best from those who would be best. How do Tiger Woods or Wayne Gretzky differentiate themselves from their competitors? It is their ability to sustain concentration in the face of stress.

What makes you good at this game is discipline, the right muscle memory, confidence in spite of stress and failure. You have to get the mechanics right and prepare. Then you have to focus with intention. You may have to train yourself to do something that is not that natural. You may have to be wrong often enough to find how to do it correctly. To succeed, you have to stay in the game even when you are not succeeding.

"The zone is not comfortable," said Sam. "Get comfortable with the discomfort. It is being a little bit on edge. Trading is a game of uncertainty."

How to Stay in the Zone

Staying in the zone is a constant process. It requires correcting your course. Traders have to learn to make distinctions between new opportunities and seeing things in the same old way.

Jordan used hard work to move out of a big hole and back into the zone. "Think about what is going on instead of freaking out about movement in the stock," he said. "Take a step back and think about what is going on. Watch the tape. You live by the sword and die by the sword. Trading is a lot of work. I am proud that I was down four million dollars for the day. It made me start working. I work hard all day long. I am exhausted at the end of the day. I was in the hole. I went home. I looked at 500 charts and read all the research reports. It paid off. I got excited. I am motivated to do it."

Jordan needs to reflect on what he did to get out of the four million dollar hole. He needs to outline it so that he doesn't forget it. He needs to develop a systematic approach to his trading. To stay in the zone, you have to take charge of making it happen. More importantly, you have to get past your own inhibitions and release the power within you.

"I have to be in the zone where I don't worry," Jordan said. "When I am worrying about my profit and loss, it takes me out of the zone. I try not to focus on profit and loss, but establish it. You have to ask yourself what you have to do to reduce the fear and increase your confidence."

The key to staying in the zone is recognizing when you are falling away and then getting back on line.

Marcus described it well. "Traders need to make small successes and build on them. Create a self-fulfilling prophecy. When you are off-center, get centered. When you are in sync you can see things better. You have to be willing to correct small pulldowns so they don't get too big."

Of course, it is often easier to make this statement than to do it. When you are facing a losing trade or a losing month, it is hard to stay on focus.

Case Study
Even self-confident traders like Jordan can have a hard time getting back into the proper mind-set when they are slipping.

Jordan was facing his only losing month last year. He didn't like the thought of facing a loss after such a successful run. "It took me a year to begin to figure out how to trade," he said. "I am up now." But he soon realized that in order to stay on track he couldn't hold on to a losing trade. " I have the confidence to stick with my convictions. To play well I have to break through limiting notions." *TARGET AWARENESS, PARKED ATTENTION, TRUST LET 'ER RIP, LET IT FLOW / GO ACCEPTANCE*

Another aspect of staying in the zone is increasing your target. Once you have your first $100,000 month, you don't want to go back to $50,000. You play at a different level. As you begin to realize more of your target, you need to set a higher goal.

"The key is to maintain a proper performance state, and the results will follow," said Marcus. "I am not willing to get thrown off course. I am willing to go through the pain of paring down. Profits flow from the profits. I commit so I don't get off the track by too much. I am not attached to the results when I am trading well. The process, the hunt, is all the enjoyment. If I can stay in that state, I will reach my goals."

Of course, entering, being, and staying in the zone all takes practice. It is a daily routine, a lifelong routine. When you get out of the zone, get back in it. As you become committed to staying in the zone, you will stay in it longer.

As the process becomes more interesting, intense, and challenging, the trader becomes more involved in the flow and more engaged in the process. Trading is no longer merely the execution of trades nor a quick way to make money but a life-engaging process whereby people can become involved totally in a research effort. When that research effort is combined with action, it puts them at risk. It is being at risk that makes for being in the flow. That is the attraction of the game.

"When the market doesn't cooperate," said Harold. "I get this sound in my ears like violins out of key. I can literally hear it. All you can do is sell or buy more. You can't make the market do what you want it to do. In the right mental state, you know the strings will come back into tune."

Trading is more than just getting a hot stock tip. It is about being engaged in a mystery, solving a problem, or piecing together a puzzle. This process totally absorbs you and requires constant and intense focusing, but it makes trading so exciting.

Chapter 2

Overcoming the Past

"I can't."

"I'm afraid."

"What will people think?"

"What if I fail?"

"I better not."

"I have to be perfect."

" I can't cry."

"I have to be self-reliant."

"I don't want anyone to know my weaknesses."

How many times in the last week have these phrases floated through your mind as you were about to make a trading decision? How many times have you gotten caught up in thinking about a decision in your past when you needed to make one in the present? These instances are your past sneaking up on you, whether you wanted it to or not. It happens to all of us. It limits us, putting the brakes on our opportunities and our dreams.

Despite their extraordinary capability for mastering the environment, human beings have a difficult time in mastering certain fundamental principles of life. A major reason for this difficulty is the enormous memory capability of our brains, which helps us to adapt and process remarkable amounts of information. But it also keeps us locked into old habits, which, in turn, keeps us from accurately seeing the reality before us. *It's POSSIBLE. THINK BIG.*

Trapped by our memories and our inclination to rely on our intellects, we are limited in our capacity to be fully conscious of the freedom and opportunities before us. In effect, we are held back by our own thinking and our inclination to perceive the world through the perspective we developed in the past. To trade consistently in the zone, it is essential to become aware of these underlying unconscious assumptions.

Identifying Past Programming

Concepts from the past keep you from being in the present. Your trading today is a reflection of life principles and the conscious and unconscious designs or structure of your thinking that was programmed in childhood. Your trading reflects your unconscious assumptions about yourself and the world—what you believe is possible, where you automatically decide to stop, how willing or unwilling you are to be fully engaged in the events of the day.

Your trading will not fundamentally change, no matter how much you try to shift or change your thoughts, until you are aware of your past assumptions. If you are like most traders, you may not be trading as if you can make a difference or as if you were responsible for what happens in your career. Rather, you are more than likely operating out of a belief system that was designed for security and survival. Although this system may no longer be relevant, it continues to keep you trapped in the past and stops you from trading in the zone.

Learned early in life, constraining life principles function as guiding templates. They affect not only your personal life but your career as well. They include such notions as the statements listed at the start of this chapter.

These principles affect how you relate to the world. Recognizing your life principles enables you to see how much they color your perspectives and responses to events. For example, given a life principle of "looking good" and "being in control," it is extremely difficult for a trader to flow with events or to be fully engaged in the moment.

These old life principles may have first been developed to protect you from stress and to mask underlying feelings of vulnerability. Although they may protect, they also prevent you from being fully in the present. Indeed, because of such life principles, you may create more of a reaction to your own reactions than would be the case if you simply allowed yourself to experience what you are feeling.

Here it is useful to consider how much your concepts limit you. Ask yourself the following questions:

- Are you limited by what you believe you can do?

- Do your beliefs hold you back from commitment?

- Do you put limits on your actions by acting in terms of "what is possible" or what you "think you can do"?

- Do you stop long before you reach your objective or set up objectives that are so easily attainable that there is no challenge to produce incredible results?

"I can't." "I'm afraid." "What will people think?" "What if I fail?" These kinds of thoughts keep people from functioning as fully as they can.

Case Study
James is a very competitive and perfectionist trader. But he is also very uncomfortable about stepping up and contributing more to the group. He is locked into specific notions about himself and his peer group at the firm. He can't see himself performing as successfully as some of the other traders because he doesn't see success as a set of skills he can learn. As long as he continues to view things this way, he is holding himself back from all that he can be.

What you *think* can have a significant impact on what you *do*. If you think negative thoughts of limitation, doubt, insufficiency, or impossibility, or negative commands like "should," "ought," and "must," they will have a negative effect on you. If you believe you cannot do something or that if you do something there will be dire consequences, it becomes extremely difficult to find the energy necessary for producing the result. Once you recognize these repetitive thoughts and allow them to pass, you can begin to define your objectives and commit to concrete results.

The thoughts you have when faced with resistance or challenges are very likely to be the thoughts that keep alive fear of failure and anxiety. The relevance of the past is that it gives you a clue to the present, to attitudes that operate consciously or unconsciously. It gives you a handle on what your attitudes may be. It is, therefore, useful to understand how your belief about what will happen based on your past experience actually colors your participation in a variety of situations. Ask yourself these fundamental questions:

- What is the programming you bring with you and how does it block your vision?
- What is it that you want to do with your trading?
- What do you need to relinquish so that you can be more fully engaged in your trading?
- What lessons of constriction and caution did you learn early on?
- What bits of early programming do you need to recognize and surrender so as to be more fully engaged in your trading?

Think about the obstacles to achieving your creative vision. Consider what you have been unwilling to give up by answering these questions:

- Are you attached to an old view of yourself?
- Do you hold on to beliefs and superstitions from the past so as to avoid anxiety?

- Are you afraid to ask for what you want?
- Are you afraid that involvement with people will deplete you of energy?
- Are you afraid that you will lose the support of others if you become engaged in a meaningful project?
- Do you believe that others will reject you if you pursue a larger vision for yourself?
- Do you believe that you will fall apart if you let go of some old notions about yourself?
- Are you attached to an incorrect notion about yourself?
- Do you use your "nice" image as a rationalization to remain passive and unassertive?
- Do you believe that you are "special," and does this belief keep you from taking some ordinary actions?

What stands in the way of pursuing your objectives? What excuses do you use when you are not reaching the level of success you wish? How much do you retreat to automatic thoughts such as:

"I don't really care what happens."

"I don't need to do this."

"I don't want to look foolish."

I am not suggesting that you can change certain fixed dimensions of your life. Obviously you can't change your height or the color of your eyes. But you can change your conceptual system and, by doing so, you can change the way you experience the world and your trading.

The solution for escaping the predicament of early programming is to live outside the limiting constraints of our intellect, habits, and past perspective. Consciously creating a goal or vision gives us a vehicle through which to sweep away past habits so that we can tap into our full potential.   VISION: ECLIPSE OUR "STUFF"

Case Study

Let's consider Thomas, who described certain childhood experiences and attitudes. "My mother's favorite brother, Jack, was a gambler. While she admired him, she always cautioned me about not following in his footsteps. I think her efforts had the reverse effect, like telling someone not to think of a pink elephant," said Thomas.

"In the '60s and '70s my uncle made and lost several fortunes by gambling. He blindly and recklessly bet on sports. He continually took shots but never measured his risk. He thought he was calculating his risk, but, in fact, he wasn't. He was hoping to get a hit. He gambled everything away. There's a lot of hope and superstition in gambling. I have never gambled. I have assiduously avoided doing anything that might be reflective of the gambler's mentality. But having said that, I think I have a bit of my uncle in me. I have the fatalism of a gambler. I take a profit too quickly to lock it in because of a fear of having things taken away. On the other hand, if I am wrong, and the stock is down a couple of bucks and is not doing what it should be doing, I am not pressing and buying more. If the stock is not acting right, I get out because I don't want more taken away from me. I am constantly defensive. I put a cap on things. Some of this is good. I keep my losses down, but I think my fear of gambling away my profits holds me back from taking appropriate and necessary risks to increase my profitability."

Can you see how Thomas's past has affected his present trading experiences? Because of the influence Thomas's uncle had in his life, Thomas is definitely not a gambler, but his fear of becoming one now leads him to hold himself back from succeeding. He doesn't push himself or his trades to the fullest for fear of self-sabotage. He plays it safe for fear that he might lose it all.

Traders such as Thomas can reach their goals by taking action consistent with them. This approach requires constant vigilance and self-awareness. These traders must be aware of their inclination to act compulsively in certain repetitive ways. They must identify the past programming that is influencing their decisions.

When a trader allows the goal to determine his size, then searches for additional supportive information to give him an edge, he is increasing his control over the outcome. He is doing exactly the opposite of what the gambler does. He is not taking a shot. He is trading from a disciplined approach to the probabilities.

Over the years I have focused on a variety of trading behaviors in an effort to expand the trading capability of traders. Robert, for example, had difficulty in starting over at the beginning of the month. Over time he overcame the psychological problem by developing a definite sense of direction, tasks to pursue, and a definite process for finding catalytic information that could be applied to short-term trading.

Some past programming that may influence your trading can be seen in thought processes that incline you to:

- Wait your turn.
- Go slow.
- Watch out.
- Get someone else's approval.
- Avoid mistakes.

As long as you are being influenced by these subconscious attitudes, you cannot do what is necessary in the next moment to reach your goals. However, you can begin to approach your trading in a more rational way. It is possible to bring a little more understanding to your trading and to enhance the way in which you function and experience your life. To become a master trader you must seek challenges, acknowledge failure, grow from adversity, stretch your capacity to undertake more complex tasks, and relinquish costly and time-consuming habits.

One of my objectives is to help you identify and understand some of the basic life principles that you developed early in life that have created limiting notions about yourself and reality. Recognizing these principles will help you change the quality of your trading by allowing you to trade in terms of a consciously chosen objective rather than in terms of the habitual perspectives programmed into you early in life.

Modifying Your Behavior

Much of my work with traders has unearthed many behaviors that seem to function like life principles. These behaviors or attitudes stop traders from being as flexible as they need to be. Without taking action to change these life principles, traders will be unable to push to a higher level of success.

[handwritten: FEAR = PLAYING NOT TO LOSE. RATIONALIZED AS PERFECTIONISM]

✓ Averting Losses

One common pattern is loss aversion or trading not to lose. Trading not to lose is a common approach and doesn't lead to real satisfaction but to sense of quiet desperation. The trader, trapped in her own self-protective habits, is afraid to put more on the line or go for broke. As a result, when she does, she is often off-kilter and loses more confidence. Even when she succeeds, someone who is trading not to lose doesn't feel terrific because she isn't getting the joy of the swing. She knows she can do better, but she has self-protectively taken herself out of the game and is often reluctant to try.

> *Case Study*
>
> James is a cautious, fearful guy who realizes that he holds himself back from major performance by virtue of his tendency to scalp and play it safe in order to keep from losing. He avoids uncomfortable feelings rather than trying to maximize his trades. He has no concept of stretching himself and trading in terms of larger targets.
>
> James is simply not swinging at the ball when he has the chance. He puts too much emphasis on not making a mistake. He has to learn that just like in the game of baseball, you can't stop playing because you strike out once. Instead, look for the good opportunities and swing again. Remember, until recently, Babe Ruth not only hit more home runs than anyone else, he also struck out more than anyone else.
>
> Until James gains more confidence about taking chances, he has to make more calculated swings. Looking for ways to enhance his trading, we talked about reducing the variety of things he was trading (commodities, currency, fixed income) and concentrating

on those items that he was really good at (currency). In this way, he could watch things more closely and remain longer in his trades. In order to overcome this fearful cycle, James also needs to monitor his moods. He needs to discover how past memories and losing experiences are getting him out of good trades. He needs to watch how he hesitates, doubts his inclination, and diminishes his willingness to take a risk in a trade. For example, he had a problem when he was getting into a dollar-yen trade where there was room to get bigger as the yen was getting weaker. James hesitated because he was locked into a low rate of return and fearful things would turn against him.

"Consider what handicaps you bring to the trade that keep you from succeeding," I told him. "Identify the patterns that are holding you back. There are times that our own humanity ruins the trade. Sometimes you have to be like a machine. Try to trade independently of the way you are thinking and feeling." *PLAY*

"It's going up. I am afraid to get in the last tick," said James "I used to want to sell it at the top. Now I don't get involved, or I sell it too soon. I might try to be a contrarian. I have been burned. I don't do it, then kick myself for not doing all I can do. I don't trust my instincts." *THE VOICE*

James can learn to play to win, but there is no way of doing it that is comfortable. "You have learned how not to fail," I told him. "You haven't learned how to win. You are not taking the shot. You have to learn to play at the level you want to play at." *ARE YOU EVEN IN THE GAME*

Loss aversion, rationalized as perfectionism, often keeps experienced traders from getting bigger. Duncan was another trader who tuned into the market swings but was not trading big enough. He tended to micromanage and overreact and not trade in terms of his objectives. He wanted to make $1 million a month, but to do this he needed to be in more than one 50,000 share position and use more of his capital. He struggled with reading the market, the Fed number, the CPI [consumer price index], and option expiration events at the end of the month. He seemed to be overreactive, tight, and struggling to get to a plateau.

[handwritten: STEP UP. PRICE CONTROL. OPERATE TO WIN. "TARGET AWARENESS"]

If you are having this problem, you need to learn how to maximize *[handwritten: PRACTICE TARGET CONFIDENCE]*
your trading. Look back to see what your best trades were, where you
made the most money with the least risk. Is there any pattern to it? Remember, it is OK to avoid trades that don't work for you and that only
make you more fearful and inhibited.

It is imperative that you use your *[handwritten: COURSE]* trading strategy to help overcome this problem. By following a strategy that you have outlined, you
will know your entry and exit points and will decide to do something
because you have decided to do it. You will not wait for the feeling that
gives you the message to go ahead. We discuss more about this strategy in the following chapters.

Rejecting a Win

Of course, some people can have almost as difficult a time accepting a
win as they do a loss. A winning trade can throw some traders off their
game and distract them from future successes.

"I am surprised by my success and am trying to enjoy it," said
Stan. "When things go very well, I am nervous that it won't last."

To prevent a win from becoming an obstacle to trading in the
zone, traders must take some of the same steps as when overcoming a
fear of losing. Remain focused. Handle your emotions. Continue taking
steps to reach your goal. Move quickly into the next trade.

Case Study
Jeffrey was a very smart and eager guy but had trouble holding on
to winning positions for a reasonable amount of time, that is, positions where his technicals and fundamentals pointed to much
bigger profit potential than he was taking. For example, he might
scalp one point in a stock that ran up 5 to 10 points. He was so
pleased he was right that he would take a quick profit.

Jeffrey needed to learn to take profits when he should and to
hold when he could. In general he was short and covering to take
profits and then shorting more into rallies. He is now trying to develop more consistency and is watching futures and the real time
P&L [profit and loss] trade entry system simultaneously on his

new computer setup, which has helped. He is also learning how to do more work on fundamentals.

Denying Reality *DOGMATIC STUBBORN LOCKED ON CANT CHANGE OR JUST DONT SEE IT.*

Another common problem among traders is denying the reality before them, especially when a stock begins to drop unexpectedly. Here failure to deal with reality is covered up by excuses and a search for reasons to justify an ultimate reversal. The trader who is less experienced easily slips into this kind of self-justification and fails to get out of a bad trade hoping things will get better.

> *Case Study*
> A pattern of denying reality was demonstrated by Ron, who always seemed to be optimistic about his trades but was not producing the results. He was doing a lot of work but had not been able to find any good ideas in the market sector he covered. He was somewhat frustrated but hoping things would get better in his group. I suggested reducing the size of his trades, shortening his time frames, becoming more agile in his trading to keep his losses down, and perhaps introducing tighter stops until things got better.

[handwritten margin note: WALK DOWN SHORT TERM FOCUS]

Following the Herd

Herding can be seen in the wide swings stocks take that reflect the distillation of millions of decisions made in the same direction. It is difficult for a trader to go against the herd unless he understands the power of the herd mentality and has an edge in terms of knowing more about a company and its stock than the rest of the world. Many novice professionals find themselves being drawn into the herd mentality of the trading room in unstable markets that are hard to predict.

> *Case Studies*
> Anthony, a relatively new trader, made a mistake by getting into some trades with the room and not doing his own work. He got caught up in the momentum of the room and didn't follow his own

guidelines in terms of sizing his position at the level that was most comfortable for him.

Another new trader, Michael, was struggling to get in the game and was inclined to listen too much to others and get talked out of taking certain positions. The solution for him was to seat himself next to an active gunslinger like Carl who could give him a lot of the push he needed.

The herding phenomenon can be a distraction for more experienced traders as well. Jerry and Harrison made close to $3 million for the month of August 1999, but were not satisfied that they had perfected their strategy yet. They wanted to make $5 million. They had consistently lost money when they got off their strategy, were too influenced by calls, and traded impulsively outside their own plans. Their model was basically working, but all their short-term decisions were wrong. They had to stop changing their theses to justify being in stocks and had to separate their long-term ideas from their short-term trading ideas.

This chapter covers the first step to trading in the zone—identifying perspectives about yourself that inhibit successful trading. Throughout this book I continue to review herding and other constraints that appear in the actions traders take every day. I discuss how overcoming these attitudes and actions can help traders learn to trade bigger and better.

The next step in reaching the zone is choosing a goal and initiating behavior consistent with that goal. In Chapter 3, you can learn how these two steps work hand in hand. The more you identify inhibiting, early-learned patterns, the easier it will be to take the steps necessary to function independently of them to reach your goals.

Chapter 3

Using a Goal

If you want to climb Mt. Everest, you can't continue to jog around the block one mile a day. You have to ask, what does climbing Everest require? Then you've got to start working at that level of preparation.

The same idea applies to trading. To succeed at it, you need to define specific goals and then begin to do that amount of work that is commensurate with your goals.

At first, the goal of a trader named Chris was too vague—"to make as much money as I can." He knew that a concrete goal of $100,000 per day was indeed realistic. Why was he not reaching it? Because he was "afraid to lose." He wouldn't ride out his trades as much as he could. He had a tendency to scalp to get a little profit. He couldn't maintain the courage of his original convictions.

We talked about using the goal as a lens through which to guide trading decisions. I suggested that if Chris consciously kept the $100,000 number in front of him during the day, his capacity to stay in a trade for a longer period of time would increase, as would his profitability. We also talked about the importance of setting up criteria and then preparing the night before.

Chris climbed his Everest when he finally realized that the goal was not a number but a lens through which to envision his opportunities clearly—on a wide screen, in color. When he grasped the idea of his goal as the beacon for making trading decisions—such as how long to remain in a trade, the size of the position to take, and the kind of work necessary for stepping up—he had the mind-set to accomplish it. He finally made it—a huge hit on 250 calls of QRS, which went up 12 points. Later in this chapter, I'll explain more clearly the process that led to his success.

Setting the Goal

A giant step in shedding constraints that lock you into the past is to trade in terms of specific goals. Although most people accept the value of a goal as an objective worth having, they don't necessarily invest it with as much meaning as a guiding principle for their trading.

It is possible to consciously select powerful and meaningful personal goals as guideposts to your actions rather than being governed by automatic personality factors. By committing to a goal and then using it as a lens for focusing all of your efforts on the process of achieving it, you will be able to tap into untapped resources within yourself. Then you can shift your attention to your future goal, which can help you to relinquish fears of the past, concerns about your image, and the opinions of others.

Goal setting is not a new idea. But what differentiates this trading approach to simply setting a goal and working toward it is the way in which you use your daily goal. Ideally, it should be used to help you plan your strategy and then to measure your performance to see what you are doing, what you are not doing, what has changed, and what you need to add to your trading. The goal gives you a focus and helps determine the size you need to trade in order to reach that target. It helps you keep playing in terms of specific increments you have previously decided upon. It directs you as to when it is time to exit a trade and take the profits or hold on longer and wait.

When setting a goal, it is important not to underestimate yourself, but also to be realistic. Excessive goals can lead to frustration, demoralization, and the loss of motivation. Traders should examine their goals regularly and adjust them as necessary. If a goal is too easily obtained, increase the number. If, after some time, it is found to be unreachable, step back and reconsider the number. Lower it if necessary. Don't see it as a reflection of yourself, but as a necessary step in improving your trading game. Of course, this process is not always easy.

"I was feeling embarrassed," said one trader. "Everyone was looking at me, especially the boss who said I was setting my targets too low, below my ability. I agree with him. I could do better."

Case Study

Consider Greg, an experienced day trader who couldn't get on a winning streak. As a result of being in a losing mind-set, he began to cut into his profits at every single step, thereby missing considerable profits.

"My batting average is not good. I am not picking the best of my ideas," he said. "Instead of doing all ten, I am picking five out of ten. I am getting involved in names. I am not staying in for the full fight. While I think it should last three days I give up on it, give up on the idea. Then two days later it goes up. I am not waiting for things to develop."

Consider this idea: If you set a goal and actually write it down, the goal will act as a point of reference for you. Put it on a sticky note and slap it next to your computer screen so it stares back at you throughout the day. Do this when you set your daily goal each morning. Save the notes from each day, writing on them how closely you actually came to your goal. Keep these notes in one place so you can look back over them at the end of a week.

Just remember, setting the goal, even focusing in on the goal isn't enough. You need discipline to keep your losses down. You need self-control so as not to get caught up in self-destructive habits.

Although Ken had developed a goal, he was having trouble using it to his advantage. "I am only halfway towards making my daily goal. In fact, having a goal makes me press my bets and sell things too soon. I have the potential to make three points in my best ideas," he said in respect to how he could reach his goal and get back on strategy. "I am only making a half point. The differential is staying in longer. That is the hardest thing to do."

A goal provides a framework from which to select appropriate actions independently of your own automatic or habitual thinking. In Ken's case, his goal should be a guidepost in helping him stay in positions longer. By concentrating on his strategy and relying on his information and conviction, he should be able to hold out a little longer in order to make bigger profits in an attempt to work toward his target. His problem is that he is too anxious to get the profit. By looking at the longer-term picture and working toward a greater goal, he can develop the patience he needs to stay with a good position.

For example, knowing he has a weakness to exit too soon, Ken can now "practice" holding a trade until he has reached a designated exit point. By following a strategy that outlines defined entry and exit points, Ken can even relieve some of the internal pressure he feels at staying in a trade longer.

The goal is designed to help you create a wide enough lens to encompass more opportunities. The implied promise of your goal allows you to create a new identity based on your verbal act. You become what you declare. You have to live up to your declaration.

The objective is to select a goal larger than any limiting self-concept that you now may have and to take action today in line with it. When you act in the present, in accordance with your vision for the future, you set the stage for liberating yourself from your past programming.

Case Study

For example, let's consider Chris, the trader we mentioned at the start of the chapter, and how he eventually conquered his Everest. He was young and smart but overly cautious. His initial problem was diagnosed as needing to hold longer. Chris had been trading for two years at the time of my first assessment and appeared to have a problem in getting bigger and thereby increasing his profitability. He tended to get out of positions quickly, but observation suggested that he needed to learn to take bigger positions and then get larger when his positions advanced.

A look at some of his statistics showed a high trading volume with small but consistent unit profitability over the year 1997. His average winning trade was $583, and his average losing trade was $417, giving him a win/loss ratio of 140. His holding period per trade was 0.46 days.

Chris's Sharpe ratio was 3.41 with a risk-adjusted return on capital of 180.98 percent. Of interest was the fact that 87 percent of his positions were long. For Chris to become a more profitable trader, he needed to trade on both sides of the market, to hold his positions longer, and to reduce the amount of his intraday trading. Given his discipline he had the potential to become a more strategic trader.

Looking at Chris's work in the first three months of 1998 revealed some improvement in his performance. His stock selection continued to be excellent. His percentage of winning trades was 54.8 percent. Since 1997 he had increased the value of positions that he took home at night, but his holding periods decreased.

While his trade size was getting bigger, he was still unable to let profits run and still had a very small ratio between his average winning trade ($1,783) and his average losing trade ($1,466). In effect he was not making much profit on his winning trades. Perhaps he was doing too many trades where he was trying "to make a half dollar, trading off the tape while keeping the investments on."

Worried that the market was going to turn, he got out very fast. At one point he made $4 on a trade that then went up $11. This fast in-and-out style of trading was consistent with the fact that he was using very little of his capital—about $700,000.

Chris also realized that he needed a sector to specialize in. He was doing more research but still kept running into his own resistance to getting bigger without more certainty. This "strength" of caution was obviously what kept him from blowing up, but it was keeping him from doing as well as he was able to do. His new goal was to find at least one good idea a day and to learn to trade bigger without being so picky and wanting to have more conviction.

Chris eventually learned to stretch himself; he held his positions longer and concentrated on maximizing profits. His return on used capital was good in relation to the room, but he needed to use more capital. In fact, at one point he got up to 90,000 shares of one stock. By the end of December 1998, he had made $290,000 in one month and a total of almost $3 million for the year. His winning percentage was 66.14 percent. His average winning trade was $2,146. Eighteen hundred was his average losing trade, giving him a win/loss ratio of 1.35.

He also learned to begin with larger positions. In fact, he is now typically lining himself up with 20,000 shares each of five stocks. In that sense he is theoretically lined up to make $100,000 per day.

Over time, Chris continued to progress. In August 1998 he made $400,000 and was daily going for $100,000. He was also beginning to learn to short positions. Overall, he started to take conscious control of the trading process. And as I stated earlier, he did see fruitful results, specifically in his big hit on 250 calls of QRS—which was his largest single day profits ever.

The value of the daily goal—be it $5,000 or $10,000 per day—is that it gives the out-of-control trader a feeling of discipline, a sense of using his skills in a rewarding way without flailing about. When you have this sense of being in charge of your destiny, you will often make more than the daily goal. More importantly, you will see opportunities in the marketplace that you cannot see when you are frightened, upset, angry, envious, or distraught because of your failings. *INSIGHT INTUITION DECISIONS ALL IMPLICITE*

Envision your goal not just as a target, but as a lens that defines the criteria for determining what must be done in the present. This lens helps you understand how to get bigger by raising the target, reframing objectives, and trading today in terms of a longer-term objective. It helps you recognize your need to learn additional skills.

Resisting the Goal-Setting Approach

Unfortunately, many traders resist setting a goal, viewing the idea as pressure to get bigger instead of as a challenge to play up to your potential. Some traders simply do not see the benefit in setting a goal. In fact, some are adamantly against it.

"If we are down 20 today, we will make it up in a few days," said one trader, expressing his doubt at setting a daily number. "We want to make one million this month—I don't know if we are going to do it."

"If we have $2.5 million in various positions in our group, I can't tell you what we will make. I know the way the fundamentals will go. We will capture all there is in that trade. In some months it may be one hundred grand. In some months it may be a million. I don't know what we will make. The point is to make money. I can't tell you how much money we will make. We want to make as much money as we can. How can anyone tell how much they will make?"

This trader is totally missing the point. His kind of resistance will only limit his growth. Nevertheless, he still argued.

"We are too early in our maturation process to set specific goals. Right now we are getting comfortable in trading around positions. It is too short-sighted to say we are going to make a specific amount. We are already putting all the capital to work in our names. We are trading around a position to give us the flexibility to continue to be in a specific stock."

"Our view is if we are short 30,000 shares of a stock and it moves down a dollar and then bounces up, to put more on. We don't know about another company—we stayed short the position. If we said we had a goal, we might not let our winners run. We watched the trend continue. If we trade around it, it is to put more on it each way. We can't have a monetary goal."

When you trade in this manner, you will never push yourself to a higher level of play. To trade in the zone, you have to put yourself on the line.

Case Study
Fred is a currency trader with an outstanding record who had never thought about the need for a concrete goal until we talked. He began to ask himself what he would have done differently if he were driven by the commitment to a specific objective rather than simply being opportunistic and waiting for events to occur.

"I want to make the easiest money in the world. I want to have an idea that is very big but that others don't quite believe in. I want to be there first, and I want to be as big as I can be. I will make nothing, nothing, and then have a huge month. I am waiting for the big fast pitch, instead of swinging for sliders, knuckleballs, and curve balls."

In fact, Fred waits for one trade to get completed before moving on to any other trades. He does not have a financial objective to push him to find new opportunities. "I will stick with my thesis until I am proven wrong by price," he said. "Then I will get out of the trade and look for another opportunity. I don't like to start another one until the first one is done. It keeps me locked into one trade. I hone in on the easiest bet. Everything else is secondary."

When you have a goal, there is a discrepancy between where you are and where you want to be that sets up creative tension and pushes you to utilize information more efficiently. You do what you need to do given that the market variables are fluctuating. Then you have to develop contingency plans to ensure that you will get where you want to be. You want to reduce the uncertainty with information, hedge your positions to keep losses down, and buy some puts. You may need to cut your losses. You may need to enlarge your positions, form teams, or hire an analyst. You find what is missing, which is what Fred needed to do.

Listen as another trader struggled with the realization that he needs to set a daily target for himself: "I am too attached to some of my names," he said. "It is human nature to get attached. I don't care if I am right. I'd rather be wrong and make money. I want to add to my winners, but I may lose back what I made. I make some, lose some. The other way may be more choppy. I probably ought to keep taking it and buy more when it drops. I probably ought to make daily profit, combine short-term and long-term approaches. I haven't made the commitment to make it every day."

Traders need to make a conscious decision to make X dollars per day. For this trader, it was not a lack of ability or opportunity but failure to prioritize commitment to his own results.

If traders don't set a number, the chances are they won't get to that number. If they can set up a number and can get there, they will likely make more. Don't be afraid to set a target even though you won't always win.

Implementing a Strategy

After you set the target, you have to determine what it takes to hit it, which is called your trading strategy. A trading strategy helps you plan how you are going to deal with different everyday contingencies. It helps you to handle the uncertainty of the market.

A plan gives you a perspective on what opportunities to look for. It also tells you when to get in and out of positions and the maximum amount of money to be made from selected trades. It helps you resist temptations and distractions and protects you from your own emotional reactions.

To develop a strategy, you must try to distinguish the facts of your trades from your emotional responses and reactive interpretations to them. Anxiety and emotional upset often keep you from objectively assessing the situation and then coming up with creative solutions.

Examining Past Trades

As a first step, you have to discover what's missing in your discipline. Start by reviewing your best trades. What worked for you? What common characteristics did your most successful trades have? Are they all in one sector? Is it a market that you are particularly interested in? Examining losing trades is also beneficial. To see how, try the following exercise.

Look closely at a previous trade that did not work out as successfully as you would have liked. Ask yourself:

- What are the facts?
- What was the specific trade that triggered your emotional response?
- What bodily sensations did you feel?
- What emotions did you feel?
- What was your trading decision in the moment of emotional reactivity?
- What were your thoughts?
- What benefit did you derive from reacting that way?

- Was this response typical for you?

- What benefit did you derive from responding the way you did?

- How could this response be linked to a life principle that has operated throughout your life?

- What alternative responses might you have made in the situation?

When answering these questions, you may discover, for example, that you are responding with anxiety to a trade, stubbornly holding on to a position to prove you were right, then getting angry with yourself and doubling-down with the hope of recovering your losses. Instead you should face your loss, take it, and cut the increase of losses, which often follows from holding on and hoping. Another response pattern you might find is that you are getting out too soon to avoid problems and then losing opportunities on the upside.

By answering these questions and examining the decisions you made, you can determine how your emotions or past programming affected the outcome of the trade. Consider what you could have done differently in this trade had you developed a plan in terms of your trading goal. What can you learn from this trade? How can you trade more objectively in the future? The purpose of asking these questions is to help you see how to enter the zone by trading consistently with a future objective.

Having asked himself these questions and assessed his statistics, a trader named Justin realized that he was far more successful when he stayed with his game plan, concentrated on picking stocks that he knew, and ran a balanced portfolio.

"My most successful trades usually take a little longer to work," he said. "My top seven trades, which accounted for half my profit and loss, were longer than a month. My game plan is now moving forward. I have learned to provide a balance between trading and investing while leveraging all the resources available to the firm."

Case Study
Rick is a scalper. He is beginning to catch on to the possibilities of achieving targets far greater than he ever did at his previous firm. He attributes these possibilities to his new firm's willingness to en-

courage people to use their capital, in contrast to other firms that discourage its use.

For the past several months, Rick has made a million dollars and thinks that he could reach his target of $8 million (if not more) for the year. He is willing to try to make $1 million a month. To do so, he has to keep playing his game of following the tape and trading actively. He cannot get caught up in too much analysis, too much reliance on the opinions of brokers, or too much attachment to his beliefs about a stock.

As a day trader, Rick benefits from doing the research calls in the morning, but in general he has a tendency to hold on too long and lose more. He thinks the market has been tough in the past few weeks and that the research calls have "sucked." He recognizes that he has a temper and that he needs to get a better handle on it. He also needs to spend less time in small cap stocks, which are trading thinly.

From our discussion, it appears that he relaxes after successful trades and gets sloppy. This pattern seems to be associated with the excitement of reaching a target, which is then followed by a letdown and loss of concentration. He needs to stay conscious and to remind himself to keep good stops and to get out when something isn't working.

The remedy for this problem is to recognize that a trade follows an arc. Once Rick has set a trade in motion and it is on target, he needs to move to the next trade and set that in motion. As his trades succeed, he therefore has no time to experience a let-down. He is moving on to the experiences of another trade.

The idea is to have a succession of targets or goals progressively coming to fruition so that you are able to sustain the psychological momentum necessary to stay in the game.

Reviewing the Results

It is not always comfortable to look at the results of your trades, especially if they are not what you want them to be. However, it is important to remember that the results are only the results and don't mean anything about you. Results only reflect how much energy or commitment went into producing them or the structure that was designed to create them. When you experience a negative trade, you need to figure out what was missing from your plan. What strategies would produce a different set of results?

Case Study

Devin demonstrated a superior win/loss ratio and extremely good trading discipline whereby the ratio of win value to loss value was better than 2:1 on a per trade and per share basis. His average win per share was $1.94, and his average loss per share was $0.82, giving him a win/loss ratio of 2.37. However, his negative correlation to holding period (which was –.23.8 percent for trades and –.21.7 percent for shares) suggested that he could enhance his profit and loss (P&L) by quicker liquidations. His average holding period for trades was 3.32 days, and his holding period for shares was 3.25 days. If he were to get out of trades faster, he would enhance his P&L.

On the surface, Devin appears to be a very seasoned and disciplined trader. However, when his trading is analyzed, we find that his profitability is negatively correlated with his holding periods of stocks. Here again, his "strength" has a negative component to it. It is the very thing that can be modified by developing a plan—with defined entry and exit points for example.

Further analysis six months later revealed that the size of his winning trades ($10,900) was smaller than the size of his losing trades ($11,000), which suggested that he had a high pain tolerance. He needed to concentrate on getting out of his losers faster so as to change the ratio between winning and losing.

It also seemed this win/loss ratio changed when he stopped trading the old economy stocks and began trading the newer technology stocks in 1999. As he did so, he increased the size of his portfolio until it was a balanced one of $50 million, as compared to $25 million in 1998. Given the volatility of technology stocks, if you beta weight it, it is like $150 million of utilities. He usually trades 50 positions, holding them for different durations. When he has big moves in stocks, he takes his profits. In 1999 his return on capital was 100 percent.

Devin's game improved. He was good at developing a plan and was very disciplined, cutting down on his losses and increasing his profitability.

"Now I understand the game better," said Devin. "I have seen more situations, know what works and doesn't work, and what gets me into trouble. I have respect for the market. I am disciplined about getting out of it and very sensitive to entry points."

Unlike Devin, most of us tend to overreact when the results are not satisfactory. Traders often want to deny their results or rationalize them away. More often than not the situation remains exactly as it was, and no new breakthroughs are produced. The real solution is to create strategies that will help produce better results.

It is best to initiate new trading behavior in those kinds of trades where actions come easily and where you are least stymied by anxiety or fear. Consider what size positions and duration of trades come easily to you:

- What can you do with little thought, effort, or resistance?
- What opportunities are available to you today to trade this way?
- What can you see regarding this vision?

Trading requires patience and responsibility to your strategy. You have to police yourself. The important thing is not to undermine your confidence. When things aren't going well, it is important not to abandon what has worked or to try radically new things. A better solution is to stick to your strategy and to review what you need to do to get back in line with it. You need to fine tune, to eliminate misguided efforts, and remain focused and calm.

Maintaining the Mental Groove

Of course, once you are on your game and playing in the zone, you can easily get off your game again. In fact, in the course of trading in terms of your strategy, your own responses get in the way.

"Studies have shown," said one trader, "that timing of the market has little effect on long-term results. The real money is made by being able to stick it out when the going gets rough. Success is more of a matter of investor behavior than it is of investment behavior."

When you are in a mental groove, you will hang in longer. You have to have the same attitude whether you have nothing or 20 million in profits. Anybody is a winner when you are winning. Can you be a winner when you are losing?

Each trader has to understand how he sabotages himself. Traders use their past experience, their perception of themselves, or the perception that other people have of them to eliminate themselves from the game. They do eliminate themselves even though there are skills in this game that are definitely learnable. Then, of course, expectations serve others. Goals serve you alone.

As you implement your strategy, you will see what stands in your way. For instance, certain types of thoughts are likely to keep alive anxiousness and the fear of failure. Do you think such things as:

- I don't really care what happens.
- I'm too big for this.
- I'm too important a person to deal with this.
- I don't need to do this.
- I don't want to look foolish.

It is important to learn to observe when you are not following your strategy and are holding back from the pursuit of your goal for fear of failure. The more you can speak your truth, the more liberated you will become. Do not be afraid to trust your instincts. Be clear about your vision, and you will slowly begin to move toward it.

Recognizing when you are thinking negative or impossible thoughts (which produce anxiety and breakdown), you can learn to shift into positive thinking, concentrating on taking actions consistent with your goal. It becomes possible, therefore, to reframe your perspective of yourself so that you begin to trade in terms of the fulfillment of your goal and the expression of your creative potential.

Restructuring Your Reactions

As Aristotle once noted, "A thing is a thing." Things and events are what they are, not something else. Yet, we tend to add our own meaning or expectations and react with disappointment when things don't turn out as we anticipated. Often, we try to make corrections to ourselves because we think we are deficient. In fact, the problem is not always about us but about the situation.

"I am out of sync," said Grant. "I don't see opportunities. This is all self-reinforcing."

It's true. In most instances, not even the events account for why you feel the way you do. Rather, you are becoming anxious and tense because of your interpretation of the event. As you separate fact from interpretation and emotional reaction, you will gain new insight into the nature of your trading. When you can distinguish the facts as facts, you will be able to create new structures for dealing with the trading events themselves.

Rationalizing Your Performance

Staying in the zone requires staying in the game. Conviction comes from playing with conviction. When you don't trade successfully, you may want to ask yourself a few questions to see how you are rationalizing your poor performance:

- Why are you not doing well?
- What more can you do to handle more capital?
- What can you do better?
- Do you rationalize your performance in terms of last year's performance?
- Are you on top of your daily P&L?

It is critical to pursue all these issues. Consistency is crucial, as is the ability to keep producing profitable days. It is less critical that you hit home runs. If you can consistently perform at a certain level it then becomes possible to raise the bar and to buy larger numbers of shares.

By developing a plan to continuously move forward to the next trade, Rick overcame his hurdle. At one point he was up $1,100,000, which was a lot more than before. He was becoming more conscious of his tendency to stop playing his game. If he stays conscious of this tendency, he should be able to get to $2,000,000 for the month.

The idea here is to help traders perform in terms of a template and independent of their own personal concerns about their "selves" and "how they look." Goal setting is a note of confidence in the trader. It is a mind-set or platform on which to stand.

If you want to make $1 million per month, you can't do it with 5,000 share positions. You have to take 50,000 share positions, and you have to do more work to strengthen your understanding of the stocks you are trading. You have to change your parameters. When you change your parameters and you still don't hit your target, look at your strategy again. Figure out what, if anything, may be missing from your strategy, your research, or your analysis. Be willing to ask for help and to be coached by others who may see things you are doing that you cannot see. Whatever you do, don't quit or abandon your goal. Use it as the beacon it can be—not as something to stifle your trading, but to encourage you to trade better.

Ask yourself, what level of play are you going to demand of yourself? You can't get there based on your level of activity at the moment. The goal-setting exercise is designed to make conscious the relationship between effort and your goals.

Staying Committed

What differentiates the superachiever from the average performer is that the supertrader sets the goal, based on nothing, no certainty or guarantees, and then determines what must be done to achieve it. He lets the external goal, not his preconditioned beliefs and preconceptions determine what is to be done and in so doing is able to tap into hidden creative energies that remain untapped until there is commitment. The strategy and the goal help protect the trader in times of problems. To be successful, the trader must remain confident in the face of repeated losses.

Great traders have the same mind-set. They take the wins and the losses and keep building on that. It is a gradual incline. They have a focused mind-set with no wavering off the path. That is the value of a goal.

"I have transposed my skills from athletics to this business," said Andrew. "It is a competitive game with ups and downs. You win and lose. You learn how to come back. Understand the rules of the game and do the work."

You can shift your thinking and perspective and in so doing begin to change the way you perceive and respond to events. In effect, you can enter the zone and begin to trade in terms of a more powerful concept based on what you know, rather than on your own limited internal programming.

Although this idea may be a bit frightening at first, the conscious decision to expose yourself to the challenge of the zone will empower you. Here practice makes perfect. The more you practice following your strategy, the more empowered you will become and the more you will become the master of your own destiny. This practice will give you the confidence, skill, and habits to help you realize your full potential.

As you change your frame of reference, your response to events will change. As you change your response to events, your trading will begin to take shape, and you will find yourself trading in the zone more often and more consistently.

Part Two

Preparing for the Trade

Chapter 4

Gathering Information

How do you know when the news and analysis you have gathered is worth acting upon? "It's a feeling," said one trader, "a smell of an idea." When a salesperson calls in the morning, the supertrader can tell as soon as he hears a name whether he can trade the stock, whether he wants to hear the story, or whether he will pass until the picture is more clear. He can make these decisions because he has a context of information based on the work he has done over time.

In a perfect world, informational material would be up-to-date and included in the price of a stock. But in the real world, there are disparities of information and perception between people that provide inefficiencies in the marketplace. The trader needs to be astute enough in his analysis of the situation that he can trade before all the news and available research is reflected in the price of the stock.

The importance of gathering news about a company revolves around the central theme of interpretation. The more research a trader examines, the more likely she is to be able to develop her own conclusions based on her own unique interpretation of the data that allow her to trade ahead of the game. A great trader does not simply ride the crest of the wave but anticipates the wave based on an understanding of the stock and the company's strategy and actions.

Master traders know the industry and talk to traders who trade the stock, analysts who study the industry, and consultants. From this background, they can extrapolate how the market will react. Searching for more information, digging deeper, and making more calls can provide great satisfaction, especially if they get an idea right and are able to trade it successfully.

For example, Aaron wants to be able to integrate his material more quickly than the portfolio managers and the sell-side analysts. His goal is to put it all together and see the "plan" well ahead of the rest of the crowd. "This approach underscores the value of fundamental work," he said. "The better you know an industry and a company, the better you can trade it."

The Need for Good Analysis

This pragmatic view runs counter to the Efficient Market Theory. The Efficient Market Theory states that the markets represent an accurate exchange of all ideas and information, that there are no inefficiencies on which traders can capitalize, and that it is buying that forces the market up and selling that forces it down. In other words, if a company reports lower than expected earnings, then that company's stock should fall. If the company announces a breakthrough in its area of expertise, then its shares should rise. Given this explanation, investors would never be able to beat the market except through luck.

However, this theory and related ones do not hold true in a practical sense. Markets, especially equity markets, are not completely efficient. Indeed, this information enables the master trader to decipher the myriad amounts of information, signals, and indicators available to anticipate price moves and to trade them profitably. Consider the previously mentioned company whose earnings were low. A well-informed investor may have thoroughly researched the company and have anticipated the drop in earnings. The same goes for a breakthrough that might be anticipated before a public announcement.

Trading mistakes can be reduced and performance can be improved with analysis. The skilled trader must pay attention to the market's assessment and try to distinguish between reality and the daily fluctuations in stock prices. As one trader stated, "Irrational players make for irrational markets." Having the right analysis can help a trader to differentiate between the wide swings brought about by fluctuating sentiment and the real value of the stock.

Case Study

I examined the profit and loss (P&L) of a team of traders—Cody and Jeremy. A close inspection of their losses revealed a lack of in-depth analysis in selected stocks, which might have prompted other trading steps.

"In XXX YYY we ignored the fact that it was the result of a merger that closed a couple of days ago," said Cody. "We bought it because of the closing. If we had done the work, we would have realized that YYY paid $1.00 a share in dividends on a $16.00 stock (7 percent is an incredibly high yield), and XXX was going to pay 20 cents. We would have known that there were a lot of guys who own YYY for the dividend who were just going to blow it out. If we'd have thought about that, we would not own 400,000 shares of this company."

Cody and Jeremy should have asked themselves whether there was anything else they could learn about the company that might influence trading activity in the stock. Then, they could have made an educated decision about the significance of the information and would have adjusted the size of their position accordingly.

"When we're wrong, it is usually because we haven't done enough work," said Jeremy. "We haven't dug deep enough. We haven't thought through the scenarios. The ideas are half baked. I don't believe in bad luck."

So, does the ability to perform correctly improve as the amount and quality of analysis improves?

"Absolutely yes," said Cody. "Information provides you with the ability in some small or large way to eliminate blowups. It frees me from the exigencies of the trading urge and gives me greater perspective on what is going on. Effort lets you develop a new interpretation that tells you that your trade is still good or to get out before you blow up. It may tell you the stock is better than you ever thought it was."

"We were long a major pharmaceutical stock. We bought 50,000 shares in the morning. The stock was up 7 'teenies.' I started calling everywhere. It was clear the wolves were baying for these drug stocks. We held that stock for seven points on the upside. The more we did the fundamental work on the company and understood the business, the key drivers and pending catalytic events, the more we realized they wanted them. That gave us confidence to stay in the trade."

As important as research is, to get to the next level, the master trader needs to develop interpretive skills so he can preemptively trade and expand beyond reactive trading.

There are ways of trading based on finding inefficiencies in information, determining risk factors, and finding ways to reduce risk. The supertrader looks for news. He watches for catalytic events. He knows what's going on in a company. But most of all, the supertrader knows how his data relate to the trading of stocks.

This interpretation involves the ability to question things, knowing when to trust your instincts and how to trade, regardless of your emotional reactivity. "Having an original perspective gives me confidence in my intuition and my reading of the price action of stock," said George. "Know the drivers. Understand the accounting issues. Be able to short the stock if the problem is greater than what anyone said. Structurally understand the company and how it is making money. Understand the business model, the nature of the industry, and whether it is solid or flimsy. Don't read things at face value. Build an actionable thesis. You can't get into the zone without analysis."

In order to get big in an investment or trade, you need to have some perspective that allows you to enter a trade earlier rather than later and that gives you confidence to get bigger and to hold longer. Gaining this perspective is the key reason for research and analysis.

Determining What Is Pertinent

News may not always cause a movement in the stock, but it empowers the supertrader to gain knowledge that may be beneficial for a future trade. Therefore, it is useful. However, the information must have some validity. A lot of information will justify taking action, but it may not be relevant. So how do you determine what is pertinent?

Knowing where the stock is and where your interpretation of developments fits in the continual dynamic allows you to build a thought process that empowers you to make the trade. You can have something to confirm your instinct.

When the supertrader reads a research report or earnings release, he tries to understand it in the context of everything he knows about the stock. He is always going beyond the data point to understand the larger trading dynamics. The master trader understands the broad implications and the intellectual argument about companies. But he is also objective and weighs the value of the company in terms of the possibility of short-term moves that develop based on market momentum (independent of the ultimate success or failure of the company). He is looking for new ideas.

"I try to generate ideas by talking on the phone, looking at the chart, picking brains. Sometimes it takes months. Sometimes it happens in a day," said Jeremy. The satisfaction I get is in the 'ping' when I hear the idea and put the position on. I get an adrenaline rush and feel pumped up when the idea is out of the box. I am enthralled by it."

The task then is to sift through material and see what fits your trading template. Consider what's relevant for each specific stock. By studying lots of research there is a greater chance you will discover all the bits that together become a great trade.

Case Study
The supertrader is able to read between the lines in terms of getting the "color" that the company is presenting. He wants to know who the critical people are at a company and the significance that has for the company. Listen to Landon talk about the information he gathered and how it affected his trades:

"BBB is a recent IPO [initial public offering], and the world is still trying to figure it out. It's in a fishy marketplace. They have to set up fabrication facilities in Taiwan. I talked to a major brokerage firm. I listened to a few days of conference calls to see if someone was just touting the stock. The stock was 48. There was no reason to think they would have anything but a positive impact on the stock. There was real evidence they had just gotten back from Taiwan. Over the next two days the stock traded down 2 dollars. It was in the Asian *Wall Street Journal* that the stock was too rich. I bought some more at the bottom. The stock went up 7 dollars. Then, it went up 13 dollars later."

Information criteria will obviously differ from trader to trader and from trade to trade. But it is possible over time to differentiate original, important information from unoriginal, unimportant pieces. A variety of criteria apply to all the various informational techniques used by traders. For example, you want to determine whether there are any events or catalysts that may move the stock in the near term. You want to determine whether it is a long-term investment or a short-term position. Another thing to consider is the reality versus perception of the stock.

It is critical to have relevant reports so as to assess what is going on in a company quite distinctly from what is being perceived about the company. The key is to determine what is real and what is not.

Of course, part of making this determination involves organization. In order to be efficient, a great trader must have a systematic way of managing the information he gathers. A practical way to manage the information is to develop a rating system to help clarify what is or is not pertinent. Cody developed one such system.

Case Study
"Our rating system has developed over time," Cody explained. "Now, trades that are in the trading account have a catalyst behind them and a short-term time frame allocated to allow them to work. Long-term ideas, if they can pass muster, can find a capital allocation in the long-term account. Anything in between will just have to be missed. The rating system works like this."

"A #1 is a trade that is going up or down in the next day or two. It's a high-conviction trading idea for which we have some analytical advantage, but it has to work soon, because we're going to tie up a lot of capital. We do not care what happens to the stock when the catalyst event occurs, because we're going to sell or cover the majority of this idea when it does. Examples of #1s include when companies are presenting at conferences or reporting earnings. The key to a #1 is the degree of conviction and the short-term horizon."

"A #2 means to start building a position because (although we don't know when), this idea is going to work. We have a catalyst on the horizon, but the timing of the stock's reaction is unclear. We don't want to wait until it is a clear #1 to buy (or sell), because we can't gauge when the stock is going to react to catalysts that will affect the valuation. We also don't want to get too big in the idea because, lacking an immediate catalyst, the idea may take some time to scale into. These ideas may work right away, in which case you have a small profit. They may become #1s, in which case you get big, or the presumed catalyst may disappear, in which case you just have to take your lumps and move on."

"A #3 is an educated bet. We like a stock because it's cheap (or dear) and we think the next move is up or down. These are market or flow trades. We do not have some shocking insight, but we like the bet on a risk-adjusted basis. Often, these trades will keep ideas in front of us while they develop. They're more marginal and will be used as sources of funds for #1s and #2s."

For the master trader, producing results is a reflection of having had all the elements come together. Producing results means being able to make the great trade by combining knowledge, information, skill, and the capacity to read the markets.

After three years of a success trajectory, the master trader can recognize when a company is failing. He reads every night. He has an arsenal of skills. He gains confidence and objectivity and doesn't read things at face value. He builds a thesis and examines the price action. He understands the company in its historical trend. He has a filter that allows him to decide what is good, what makes sense, and what is relevant. All these factors converge in being totally in the moment.

Processing the Information

René Descartes said, "Seek simplicity but distrust it." Do the simple things without being simple minded. If you distill it to the wrong things, you'll be wrong. That being said, how do you intelligently find new analytically relevant information that hasn't yet been disseminated that allows you to predict the direction of movement of a stock? You need to be able to determine the impact of the news on the Street's perception of the stock. It is a multifold process.

It is useful to look for undervalued stocks where new, potentially profitable developments haven't been incorporated into the price of the stock. These developments provide potential perception changes that have yet to be recognized by the Street.

The skilled trader is listening with the "third ear" for changes in opinions or estimates. The analysts do not call and say, "We have this number and we are going to do this." They write up a report, do a break-in call on their squawk box, and issue First Call notes to disseminate their change of opinion. They might relay the financial numbers. They may say, "Have you heard about the new numbers?" They may give some opinion and some revision.

"I want to anticipate what the analysts are going to do," said Jennifer. "I can tell whether news is good or bad in terms of its affect on the Street or the way traders will respond. Balance sheets are not critical to me. What is important is how business is now. You need to spend as much time as possible figuring out who is doing well and who is not. I know what's important and what will move stocks. As I have traded longer, I am trading bigger. My confidence has grown as I have understood more."

Listen carefully to what your associates are saying. Listen for the conviction in their voices. You can tell when people are really convinced of the value of something, even when they don't know that they are conveying that conviction. Being able to decipher subtleties in their communications is the skill of listening to the way people communicate.

The master trader is alert to what the masses think and therefore is able to use their trading as countertrend signals. In this way she stays in the game and does not get too preoccupied with her own performance. This goes along with her efforts to keep looking for new trends and how others may be misinterpreting the trends. It allows her to keep expanding her goals and maintaining her commitment to excellence.

For example, the master trader knows that traders off the floor tend to take long-term positions instead of scalping fractions, as is true for traders on the floor. She knows that when upstairs traders buy big, it is a good signal. She also knows that the greater the volume of the specialists shorting relative to the public, the greater the odds that prices will subsequently fall. Elaborating on this perspective one analyst told me, "The master trader is inclined to compare trading activity in the first hour versus the last hour of trading. The more sophisticated traders tend to trade in the last hour of a session (when the market is down) while the irrational investors trade more in the first hour of trading (when the market is up). That's a sign that there is a distribution going on by smarter investors. When the market is down in the morning and up in the afternoon, that means the smarter investors are accumulating." While these generalizations aren't always true, they do provide a framework about looking at overall trading patterns in the market.

"When you know you are right, and the stock rips back in your face, it suggests there was more information out there or that people don't care," said Mandy. "That is the discomfort. If it doesn't come easy, then you aren't sure. If everyone else seems sure, it may create more uncertainty for you."

For example, Blake traded a major cyclical company based on a call that sounded interesting. He bought it at 53 and sold it at 40. There was the possibility of it being acquired by a French company, and the previous quarter there had been a controversy.

"There was no reason for me to trust this company," he said. "I didn't know the players. I didn't do an independent analysis. The lesson I learned was not to trade that big unless I know the players, and I am better off visiting companies, having relationships with analysts and buy siders. The critical variables keep changing. So, you have to continually modify your view."

"When the market rallies, you have to know what will move. Why are certain groups moving while others are not? You need to have a thesis, for example, that the money will come out of the financials. Where does the money go then? If people are warned about growth, it should move into the basic growth companies such as cyclicals. The savvy trader also pays attention to interest rates."

Information is more than just simply saying that there is a seller out there or there has been some random stock market movement. It's useful to know what is going on with news events and significant catalysts. It's also useful to find out how many people want to sell two million shares and how many people have 50,000 shares to buy or vice versa. There's a lot of different events to help you decide to make a move. There are significant dates or reasons for acting because something is happening tomorrow. Everybody knows the same things pretty quickly. You need to have an idea of what's going on without chasing after a stock.

It is also important to get a feeling for historical valuations relative to interest rates that can sometimes help you to grasp the market's fair value. Try to get a handle on supply and demand characteristics within the marketplace and stock offerings relative to stock buybacks. Be aware of the differences between sectors and industries and the subtle kinds of fundamental analyses that are necessary to understand different groups of stocks.

Who is trying to do what, why, how much, and when? What is the story and what does it mean? There is always someone else on the other side of the trade, and it is useful to determine what he is thinking. Ask the following questions:

- Why is the price where it is?
- What has caused the volume of trading to drop?
- What is going on in the company, in the macro picture, in the markets?
- Why is the brokerage firm buying shares of this company?
- Why is another brokerage firm selling?
- Why is the managing partner buying or selling the stock?
- Why is the other guy selling?

You want to consider these questions when you are thinking of trying to do the opposite of what everyone is doing. Remember, it is critical to understand the complexity of companies and the drivers. Determine what is new about the new companies in order to be prepared for trading, especially in the new Internet and technology spaces that came to the fore in the middle of 1999.

The importance of such understanding was illustrated by the development of DSL (digital subscriber line) technology, which allows transmission of data on existing copper lines in excess of speeds currently available using dial-up access. With a minimum of infrastructure built out at the local phone company office, it was possible to develop huge companies worth billions with a minimum of revenues. In 1999, these stocks ran up very fast because of demand and not enough capacity to price it. It was a classic early phase phenomenon that provided a high risk-reward ratio for those traders who were in on it in the early part of the curve.

Digging deeper for material about a company helps you know what to trade bigger and where to add when it is going against you. Having a good story can produce a real impact. Each of your movements should be explainable and have a significance that can be factored into making future trading assessments.

Case Study
Forrest's basic approach to analysis and his search for inefficiencies is linked to his trading strategy.

"Analyze information and its effect on the perceptions on the Street so as to predict actions likely to be taken by traders vis-à-vis particular stocks," said Forrest. "The perception of change is what I am looking for. If the Street is looking at something in a certain way, and a news event will change the perception, I need to know the Street's view of things. That is reflected in the price. Will an event change the view on the Street? I want to anticipate this before others."

Since he spends considerable time assessing the impact of events on the trading of stocks over an intermediate range of time, Forrest prefers to establish a few positions and trade the market based on his information. He prefers an in-depth approach to a handful of stocks over a cursory approach to a lot of stocks. Since his strength is understanding the dynamics of a company, his research approach to companies is most consistent with a longer-term portfolio style of management. He likes getting the First Calls for information to test and trade them. He believes in research, setting an objective, building the position, and having the discipline to get out. With his talent for interpreting information, he is well suited for building this kind of approach to trading.

The more you have to work with, the more decisive you can be in your decision making too. Translate the call. Trade ideas.

It is vital to know when your analysis is strong enough to enable you to put a big bet on. "It is the one in three trades that you feel like moving on," said Brandon. "When you feel that confidence, you have to use it and really push things. Sometimes you have to use discomfort as well. When you are sluggish, you have to slow down and reassess."

You need to follow this kind of thought process to be able to position yourself for major market moves. Remember that the game is always different, and the critical variables keep changing. Allow the signposts to help you. Get in and trade to test your hypothesis and then adjust accordingly.

Even when you have done a good analysis of the company, you must also factor in the sentiment on the Street. Figuring out there may be an inflection point in changing that perception are critical factors in a successful trade. Your ultimate choice is based on a combination of factors. Having the fundamental figures, you might still act contrary because of your analysis of the Street and what the market will do.

In addition, your analysis does not prevent you from experiencing the swings in stocks that result from market action independently of fundamentals. Therefore you also need to consider other, often more subtle, clues.

For example, Chip followed the calls in seven oil stocks but didn't pursue his own observations of related parameters such as the situation in Indonesia and the price of crude in the 1997 crisis. He lost big in all seven stocks. He recognized that the calls were good, but he didn't use his own judgment and was caught flat-footed.

In addition, some traders do not benefit as much from gathering information. Day traders and tape traders simply don't need such reports to conduct trades because they are trading momentum, trends, and charts and not so much the fundamentals of a company.

Beyond the gathering of fundamental information about a company such as balance sheets and income statements, the trader also needs to view information not only for its intrinsic value but in terms of its relevance to what other traders are likely to do. He needs to ask additional questions beyond the analysis. He may even want to take a course in finance or read some books in order to be able to learn basic business concepts critical for understanding the underlying dynamics of the companies he is trading.

By incorporating news gathering into your overall strategy and piecing the puzzle together in an organized fashion, you can use the information to develop an actionable thesis on which to build successful trades. However, there is another important component to making information work for you—timing.

Timing Is Important

The trader's challenge is to time the information in the context of other things that he knows about the stock and its trading pattern. He has to keep assessing a wide variety of data to find which information is significant at a particular period of time. Information may not be pertinent six months from now.

"There were a lot of good ideas this month, but my timing was not opportune with what the market was doing," said Forrest. "I had great ideas and good fundamental reasons to be in them. But when you buy it, the stock goes down because of market pressure. This consumes a lot of energy."

Sometimes when you are early and the stock is not acting well, you are scared out of it because not enough people are trading it yet. There are always overreactions. Some jump on the bandwagon late and ride it further.

So, if you act on the material too early, it can hurt you. If you have it too late, it can't help you. The key is timing the trade based on your analysis of the data, recognizing that the value of the analysis decays over time and may be factored into the price of a stock.

Ideally you want to begin trading just before the information influences the analysts to make their recommendation. To do this you want to be aware of catalysts such as earnings reports, conferences, and analysts meetings, where critical information may influence the price of stocks.

For example, in pharmaceuticals, stocks react to different things at different times. At one point, prescription trends on a weekly basis may be critical. Another week, it may be the economy. Generally it is what the crowd is focusing on for whatever reason. It may not even have any intrinsic meaning but is still something to be aware of.

"One day, the group just got killed and nobody knew why," said one trader. "All of a sudden S&P [Standard & Poor's] earnings were going up. So, it made cyclical stocks more attractive than drug stocks, and people were selling the drug stocks. Large institutions like Fidelity and Putnam are able to make the big bets to move the stocks. When they decide to, they can move a group. Over time you get better at deciding on the relevant variables and news events."

"Stocks have a positive bias upward. If they double, it takes time. Ideally, you should be trying to catch the inflection point. If it has been sideways, you want to catch the initial thrust. In short-term trading you are looking for an event that will produce a positive or negative inflection in the stock and to find a stock trading at the bottom of its range where the events are meaningful and predictive of moves. You buy enough stock to make a meaningful amount of money and a few points of profit. You are looking to know the stock well enough so that at the bottom end of its range, the story is still valid."

Case Study
A common problem of beginning traders is the inclination to get into a trade too soon. For example, Forrest jumped into the paper stocks before the Fed announcement to raise interest rates 25 basis points on August 24, 1999. Instead of moving up, as he expected, the prices went down, and he lost money.

Forrest's mistake was anticipating the market's response instead of waiting to see how the market would respond to the Fed rate hike. The more experienced trader usually waits for the tape to tell him which way to trade. When it is moving in a direction that he understands, he gets into the trade. When it continues to go his way he adds to his position. In effect, he presses his bet "when the tape tells him" he is right.

In all fairness, according to one skilled observer: "It is not so easy to trade in anticipation of a Fed rate hike. At best it is a 50-50 luck bet, not a skilled trade. Forrest was simply wrong. In such instances even experienced traders get caught because they cannot afford to wait to see what happens because the trades in response to the Fed rate hike happen so fast. So I wouldn't be too harsh with Forrest."

In another instance, Forrest wanted to get into a major telephone company that was following a trend line and holding a support level, but it "got too big too quick." He was reluctant to pay the higher price and therefore missed the trade. His attachment to a price kept him from following the tape action and getting into a trade. In the first instance, his attachment to his thesis led him to act impulsively. In both examples, Forrest's own ideas took on more significance than the signals he was observing. If Forrest had followed his signals more closely, his timing would have been more accurate. The signals should have been the impetus to action.

The right time to trade is when the stock is making its critical big move. Know about trends in the industry. Eighty percent of the move takes place in a small space of time. Stocks move in a band. If you can sandwich the band you can minimize your losses and make good profits by trading the strength and weakness.

Successful trades happen when the trader has a unique perspective relative to the rest of the market. This perception, based on his analysis of data that confirms his hypothesis, gives the trader the necessary conviction to get bigger in his positions. It may be that he has anticipated a major inflection point. It may mean that he understands the dynamics of the company or the company's business model and is able to bet in terms of the company when others are responding to rumors and taking action in the opposite way. Whatever it is, it is where his research really pays off, and he can build a big position, including buying dips, buying the stock at lower prices instead of selling off, and preparing for the opportunity to make the big hit.

As one trader said, "You don't wake up in the zone. You have to work to get there."

Chapter 5

Understanding the Analysis

In high school if you had been forced to memorize every page of your American history textbook, you (and the rest of us) would undoubtedly have flunked the course. You would have felt overwhelmed, over-matched. There would have been just too much information in that book for you to absorb. So, what did you do to pass that course?

If you're like most of us, you skimmed the text. And while you were reading, you filtered out less important information and under-lined what you thought were the fundamentals—the key facts, dates, and people. Then, when you took a test, you called upon your memory of that highlighted material. You synthesized it in your mind and an-swered the questions.

Just as with your history book, there is far too much data in today's finance and economics for anyone to know it all. You can nar-row it down by choosing sectors, but still the amount of information can be enormous. It's up to you to allow your mind to skim the free flow of information and then to filter out the less important material while mentally (or physically) underscoring the most valuable pieces of data. It's those pieces that add up to your fundamental analysis of a company and its stock, and they can make the difference between being a run-of-the-mill day trader and trading in the zone.

To begin piecing together this puzzle, traders need specific tools by which they can search for and separate the vital information from the nonessential. Although each trader has a different method or a favorite resource, this chapter is devoted to some of the analyses and indicators that can help you make such determinations.

Using Technical Analysis

One tool is known as technical analysis—the examination of charts and patterns that represent price movements and volumes of trades. With the use of technical analysis, the trader can strengthen his conviction and further support his hunches about the direction or range of movement regarding specific stocks.

Prices often change with dramatic swiftness or in terms of sharp discontinuities. Even when there are minimal jumps, price change does not occur evenly over time but tends to concentrate in short turbulent periods. These price moves occur in bursts and patterns that have some regularity. A trader can assess what happened over the last several years by examining charts that graph these patterns.

Technical analysis, therefore, is useful for determining breakouts or breakdowns of different patterns. The technical analyst follows trends and momentum and is able to identify moments of price exhaustion. Classical technical analysis patterns include an inverse head and shoulders pattern (three peaks with the highest being the middle one), which is a bullish signal; triangle tops (progressively lower peaks and rising bottoms), which is a bearish signal; and a broadening bottom, which is also a bearish signal.

Although technical analysis has been criticized as trying to find "order in the midst of seeming chaos," like most tools it can be useful if applied correctly. Using this method of analysis, a trader can look at the volume of trading to find entry points. If for example, there are tons of sellers, it may be time to buy a stock or wait because it is close to bottoming. He also can consider what changes have occurred in pricing and how that is going to affect the stock. Technical analysis can provide a means by which the trader can improve his trading of indices, clarify his directions, gain clues to trading a particular stock, and learn more about specific industries.

Technical patterns do not tell you what is going to happen next in the market. Rather, they reflect various forces that have impacted stock movement in the past and may provide you with some perspective on probable trends.

Examining Technical Indicators

What are some of the critical variables or indices used to assess the market? The most important variables are interdependent rather than independent variables so that each is reflective of the others. Nevertheless, at certain times some variables are more prominent and significant than others, and the master trader is able to discern this difference. There are various technical indicators that measure some market phenomena and can be usefully applied to understanding the nature of the markets and the environment in which stocks are trading. Each indicator provides more information as part of the mosaic of assessing the stock market.

Price Action

In the old paradigm, the more a company earned, the more its stock would rise. Under the new paradigm and according to some traders, the more a company loses, the greater its stock value. At least, it seemed that way for a while. The crash of April 2000 suggested that the new paradigm might not be true after all. In 1999 the Nasdaq index was up 80 percent for the year and 48 percent in the last 10 weeks of the year. This new paradigm was revealed in the Internet-driven high technology stocks that captured everyone's attention in 1999. Some people have considered this a millennium melt-up. Fifty-seven of the year's new issues were ranked among the 200 largest technology companies in the country as measured by market capitalization. What is interesting is that most of them had minimal, if any revenues, no profits, and yet their share prices continually soared since their introduction until the big Nasdaq reversal in March and April 2000.

Over time some of these stocks predictably collapsed when it became apparent that their business models were not going to work. We had witnessed irrational exuberance, which by April of 2000 was starting to abate. No longer were these companies being valued in terms of their growth potential as they had been in 1999. More and more they were being valued in traditional ways in terms of earnings.

Whether or not the old paradigm regains favor, it's still possible to tell direction from the activity of the big institutional buyers. In the last day of the quarter, they buy to improve their performance. This drives prices up. The next day they sell these positions. Some traders lean into these, shorting them on the last day near the end of the markup. When they crumble the next day, the traders are often able to profit.

Some trades are based on a reading of the price action. After the Dow had its most significant move up the week of March 16, 2000, some traders expected the old economy stocks to gain favor once again and planned to buy these stocks on the next pullback to capitalize on another rally. They also planned to short the new economy or tech sector stocks into a rally to capitalize on the next decline.

Price action is a valuable indicator of stock activity, but according to Delbert: "Price action can freak you out. I have had situations where the price action didn't confirm what I knew, and I got scared out of my fundamental position and didn't take the big position. This might happen at an inflection point. Most people wait for a confirming view of the stock price, but then when it moves they do not want to pay up for it, since they failed to get in earlier at a lower price based on their fundamental assessment. I have to come up with my variant perception. If something radical happens that challenges my view, I have to make my bet or recognize that things have changed."

200-Day Moving Average

Are stocks too expensive? Do some technical analysis and compare the current price to the average price over the preceding 200 trading days (i.e., the 200-day moving average). As a general rule of thumb, stock prices do not deviate from the 200-day moving average for an extended period of time. If they do, you can expect some kind of correction. The problem is determining the point of inflection, the point at which the market will change.

This moving average provides a clue to determine which stocks have advanced beyond what is warranted by their fundamental value. In effect, some move high because of the movement of the markets. Others move ahead because of some inherent value. The job of the trader is to try to assess these variables to create meaning from the technical data.

The 200-day moving average is also useful for gauging the overall market. Seventy-five percent of the stocks in the S&P 500 index were trading above their 200-day moving average in May 1998. If 80 percent of stocks are trading above their 200-day moving average, the market is overbought. If 20 percent or less are trading above the average, then the market is oversold.

Therefore, as the number of stocks hitting new highs decreases, the number of stocks trading above the average will also decrease. If the number is decreasing, as it has been, it suggests the market is cooling, but the decline can take some time—up to a year. Of course, there may be a short-term correction, which means it can drop and then rise again. While many of the theories about 200-day moving average have been challenged by the remarkable bull market of the last seven years, there is still some value in considering this technical indicator in an overall assessment of the market.

Other Indicators

Whole books have been written regarding the variety of indicators that traders can use to assess the market. We simply do not have the time or space to cover them all. However, there are two other indexes that I want to mention by way of underscoring the kinds of economic numbers you want to watch. They are included in the following list of economic indicators:

- The CPI (the Labor Department's consumer price index) is a measurement of prices paid by consumers for retail goods and services. It indicates the ability or inability of producers to pass higher costs to the consumer in the form of higher prices. It is released in the middle of each month and can drastically move the markets when the numbers are above or below expectations.

- The PPI (the producer price index) measures prices paid by producers of wholesale goods and services. It is closely watched for its relationship to inflation in consumer prices. It measures three stages of production—crude, intermediate, and finished goods. Crude and intermediate prices are good indicators of pipeline inflation, but finished goods prices are closest to the consumer.

- The Labor Department's employment report is released on the first Friday of every month and is based on data from the previous month. It is an indicator of employment and wage growth and provides four pieces of data: nonfarm payrolls (jobs), the unemployment rate, the average hourly wages, and the average workweek.

- Gross domestic product (GDP) measures the total output of goods and services in the U.S. economy. The Department of Commerce issues a quarterly report on the GDP, which is considered to be the most comprehensive glimpse of the U.S. economic growth. This report sums up the consumption, investment, government spending, and net exports. It also includes a direct measure of inflation called the *GDP price deflator*, which is a measure of the overall level of prices in the economy.

- The productivity report is released by the Department of Labor on a quarterly basis. It measures output per worker hour and worker compensation costs per unit of output produced.

- Also released quarterly and published by the Labor Department, the employment cost index measures wages and benefits for hourly and salaried workers. Its measures include retirement, social security, vacations, and health insurance.

Again, this is not an exhaustive study of all the numbers or sources of information out there. In fact, it is the opposite. It is a very narrow listing of what is available. My purpose is to encourage you to find the best tools to unearth the information you need to fulfill your goal. By staying informed and prepared, you are more capable of making accurate—not emotional—decisions.

Understanding Macro

By now I hope I have made my point clearly. There is a lot of work you can do to raise the level of your game to that of the zone. One more set of variables to consider, which are already familiar to anyone who keeps abreast of world events, are the macroeconomic (macro) variables. Macro traders focus on broad themes like global economic issues and most often play them through currencies, bonds, and commodities. To the extent that these issues also affect the price of individual stocks, understanding the larger macroeconomic picture can enhance your interpretation of earnings, increase your confidence, enable you to trade equities more aggressively, and maximize your profitability.

Understanding macroeconomics adds a framework for the trader to make sense of all the information she is gathering. Macro issues have specific relevance for understanding multinationals, interest rates, and the flows of currency and for providing general perspective about market forces.

"Macro is relevant to equity traders. Its themes are usually derived from economic data and policy responses to that data," said Margaret, a brilliant economist for a major long-term hedge fund. "Your economy is the big picture. If it is slowing down, economic data tells you it is slowing down. Then you have a policy response to that data such as the Federal Reserve, fiscal policy, or currency policy."

"There is also global macro," she continued. "I look at the whole world—Europe, Asia, emerging markets. They each have data, policy responses, and equity markets. All these places are connected. For example, Asia is booming now because they are exporting to the United States. That means if the U.S. slows down, Asia will slow down. So, you can have a policy response in the United States that impacts Asia."

In different phases, the market focuses on different things. Therefore, you also need to consider other worldwide events. Macro encompasses everything that relates to the stocks. The reason you need to understand macro issues is to be able to decipher what may impact your markets.

With a short-term trade, consider what will be the next thing that people will focus on. For example, everyone wanted to know whether there would be a slowdown because of Y2K? Would it cause a recession? Were these concerns valid or a projection of fear?

Susan looked at these issues in October of 1999. She didn't believe the world was as bad as everyone perceived, but there was no clarity.

By November, the market was not at bottom. That gave her the clarity she needed.

Information is basically used to confirm intuition. You sense where the market is going and how a stock is going to do. The additional information is designed to increase your confidence, to test your hypotheses in the light of new information, and ultimately to reduce your risks. These various uses of information are the reasons for adding a macroeconomic view to your arsenal.

Assessment of a company must be done in the larger context of the state of the market. The master trader will have a broad market view and then a specific sector view. There are so many divergent macro events influencing the market that the smart trader must assess these factors and, with that as a background, must still focus on the specific companies he is trading. Remember, there is always a macro picture to consider when assessing the significance of fundamental information, and you have to decide each time which are the most relevant factors, for example, fundamentals, catalytic events, or macroeconomic factors.

Case Study
The "oil patch" is a particularly good sector to examine because of the diversity of trades it offers. Sometimes trades are based on company fundamentals, sometimes on catalytic events like earnings announcements, and sometimes on macroeconomic issues such as OPEC policies and worldwide rates of crude oil and interest rate tightening by the Federal Reserve. The master trader must weigh all these factors in determining the highest probability, lowest risk bets.

In the early part of the year 2000, Jacob discussed a complex strategy for shorting oil drillers, which took into consideration such macroeconomic factors as a raising of interest rates, an excess supply of oil inventories, and capital expansion—all of which suggested to him that the stocks were overvalued.

Jacob explained: "I am shorting oil drillers. I think there will be a significant downdraft in these stocks. The drillers prosper when big oil stocks like Texaco and British Petroleum are building wells. This was especially so in 1997 when these stocks were flying. Cap ex (capital expansion) kept going up. We got to a peak valuation on cap ex. It has been going flat to slightly up. The sell side is saying we are very bullish, and that we are at an inflection point. I totally disagree."

"Crude oil is trading at an all-time high, close to $30 a barrel. A tightening of interest rates is expected, and OPEC is having a big meeting in March. We are taking the contrarian bet while others are expecting OPEC to lower the price of oil, which should have a positive effect on the oil stocks."

"This is why I like it. Everyone is in this bet. We started shorting it one month ago, and then they fell like a stone. Now they are going up, and we are shorting more. We are getting better prices than last month. There is a seasonal factor. We will see this work by next week. We have a few macro catalysts. If Alan Greenspan puts a kabosh on growth, then you don't want to own oil stocks, and we should short some more. That's why I am shorting more now."

How could macro indices such as oil service stocks, crude oil prices, and an anticipated meeting of OPEC be used to make a macro bet on oil stocks and oil service companies? One reason to buy oil stocks would be whether OSX (Oil Service Stock Index) was tracking the higher rates of crude oil prices that was anticipated to go lower with the OPEC announcement of increased supplies being made. Anticipating the OPEC announcements, the smart traders would line up to buy oil stocks with the expectation that the prices of the oil stocks will go up.

Looking at Bonds

Bonds are another set of indicators that will tell you how the market is performing and provide perspective for you as an equity trader. According to Ralph, who specializes in trading bonds, "Their price can be used as an indicator of where the market is going. The bond market trades off event risk, technicals, and value trades—where was the historical spread—in a two-year sector. But there is a correlation between the financial sector and the bond yield curve."

He elaborates: "The yield curve is the relationship between the yield on government securities and their time to maturity. Generally, the longer-term maturity treasury notes of 30 years provide a higher yield than those of shorter maturity—one year, five years and ten years. But occasionally there is an inverted yield curve, where the yield is greater on the shorter-term notes than the longer-term notes."

"This factor," he continues, "is the reason to keep an eye on the bond market. If the yield curve changes, it may affect certain stocks in certain ways. For example, say the bond market pricing started tightening, then the stock market might start getting hit a little bit too. By watching the bonds, a trader can notice basic correlations that will help give him an edge."

"I think the theme of watching the bond market is to watch swap spreads and the trend of high-grade corporate bond yields versus the U.S. Treasury of the same maturity," said Ralph. "One year ago a ten-year maturity Ford note was trading about 75 basis points of more yield than the ten-year Treasury note. Today that relationship is 150 basis points. That shows that economic uncertainty is still growing, and liquidity is poor. When that theme starts to reverse, the stock market will scream in a broad-based rally. When will that be? When the Fed is done tightening."

Listen as Dennis gives some insight into this indicator. "Long bonds are in some ways the fixed income market's longest duration asset and the market's best reference point for what inflation will be in the future."

"Bonds are the most accurate reflection of future inflation. When the bond market loses confidence in the Federal Reserve's ability to manage inflation, the yield goes up a lot. Traders should pay attention to bonds because all stocks discount future streams of earnings by a certain interest rate."

"The bond tells you to what degree inflation will erode the earnings of companies over the next thirty years. As of August 2000, the yield curve is inverted, which means that the short interest rate is higher than the long rate. This situation tells you that the bond market expects inflation to be lower in the long term than the short term. This situation may be bad for equities since it suggests that, in the short term, the Fed may tighten interest rates. Certainly they have been bringing the short rates up over the past year because of a strong economy. If the interest rate goes up, future cash flows will be less. This will lead many traders to sell stocks."

Case Study

In September 1999, there was fear of the Federal Reserve raising rates, and therefore there was a lot of anxiety and uncertainty in the marketplace. This situation was not dissimilar to 1994 when the Fed was raising rates to put pressure on the market. They kept them down, but there was a long period of fear and uncertainty and then a rally at the end of the year. It created an enormous volatility that reflected the fear. It hopped and skipped depending on where you were.

The market was fragmented for bonds. They had turned positive on high-grade bonds. Liquidity was not what it was before. There was less money coming into the market. The resting bids were down. There was confusion.

"We're at 10,500 Dow," said one trader. "To have a consolidation and pullback at Dow 10,500 and to feel confusion is a telling thing for the long-term benefit of the stock market. Some of the confusion derives from the conflict between the raging bulls and bears. The bond market is terrible, and I am trying to hit base hits and line up for big hits. I will look for short moves. Right now, you get paid for buying them when nobody wants them and selling them when everybody wants them. But the bid offer spread is killing them."

Different Interpretations

Different people perceive what is going on quite differently. For some people it is noise. Others play the noise, which is an art in itself. Stocks trade based on emotions. People buy more when the market is moving up. The stock market therefore becomes an emotional machine.

According to one observer, "It is interesting that in a room full of traders, few have the same thought process or the same perspective on the macro events going on."

But, there are technical tools that function like a compass and act like a baffle to dampen noise. Evaluating the markets is like solving a big puzzle. The markets keep changing. The satisfaction is getting the puzzle right and making a lot of money. To do so, the trader needs to assess all these measures and never become ensnared in them.

"You have to stay focused on a day-to-day trading basis and keep looking for opportunities. Remain aware of macro events but don't get caught up in them," said Bob.

If you hit the ball correctly, the trajectory and speed will be right, and you may get a home run. But getting the mechanics and the muscle memory down takes preparation. Then you have to focus with intention as well. You may have to train yourself to do something that is not that natural.

Traders need to pay attention to who is buying or selling, the momentum, and what the value is. Value is a subjective measure. If you know a stock is going to miss its earnings, you have to know why people own the stocks. Try to understand the valuation. Why is it cheap or expensive? Know the valid catalysts. Missing earnings is not enough to short a stock.

It's also important to assess who the players are in particular stocks. If a value guy owns a stock and the company says it will miss earnings, he won't sell it. He will buy more. A momentum trader responds differently to the same information. You have to keep looking for isolated pockets of activity to determine where the action is coming from. Like an amoebae, the master trader responds differently to different situations—searching out the relevant information he needs for each individual trade.

Much like the mission of economics, which is description, prediction, and control of economic forces, the trader's mission is description and prediction of markets and control of his behavior when trading. What drives the market is fear and greed. You need to find an edge. If you think you know where the market is going, trade the market. If you can find an edge specializing in a group of stocks, trade that group of stocks. But remember you can't trade in a vacuum.

Chapter 6

Learning More

So, how much information do you need to get a jump on the rest of the pack? Let's be frank. You need an enormous amount, from a vast array of sources. And, you need to do your analysis early. But you need to understand not *just* a company's numbers, not *just* its share price movements, not *just* the opinions of its analysts, and not *just* the industry itself. You also need to know the psychology that drives the market for that stock. Sure, you need fundamental data, but you also need to be smart about the invisible, underlying variables—what is going on in the minds of those who make up the herd of other traders. You need an edge.

"Knowing the rudiments of economics are important, but developing a feel for why a company will do better or worse from tangential information is the benefit of your hard work," said Ted. "Stocks trade in a world of ebb and flow supply versus demand dynamics. The market pays more for companies with positive events as people think this management will produce more 'positive' surprises and destroy earnings disappointments. Knowing a company, its history, and the in-happenings of a group, getting a 'feel' for the change of information and valuations and how that will impact the demand side of the equation (do you buy some or short some?)—that is your edge. How you build the confidence, information flow, and ability to capture that edge is the secret."

Gaining an Edge

A trader builds his confidence by increasing the amount of fundamental work he does, bolstered by an understanding of technical indicators. While this may seem obvious, it isn't. Too many traders, even professional ones, don't fully realize the amount of preparation required for true trading success. They don't understand the kind of thought process required to make sense of the vast arrays of data available.

Information isn't available only to those trading in the zone. Most analysts and traders have access to the same information. So, what is it that is to differentiate you from all the others? What are the factors that can help you use this information most effectively to trade in the zone? Let's outline three simple steps regarding information and trading in the zone:

1. Constantly look for information and reevaluate the fundamentals against the market movement of the stock, the sector, and the tape in general.

2. Move out of "bad" positions if the stock is going against you, even if the fundamentals still appear good. This keeps your losses down.

3. Take your profit in line with your daily target. Trade the intraday volatility and news events. Trade a shorter time horizon that is governed by your target.

The last step is paramount. Being in the moment does not mean shutting off stimuli but allowing it in while you are still focusing on the most important thing—the ball in motion, the sweet spot in time. All the information you gather must be used as a means of making decisions that are related to following your strategy and achieving your goal.

"Once you have the fundamentals, you tweak it to get the edge," continued Ted. "You work harder. You have to think about it. Keep examining your good trades. Understand what you did that worked. Know the basics but then analyze the significance of the data in terms of predicting high probability likelihoods of stock performance. It can't be random execution. It has to be disciplined."

In-depth assessment is part and parcel of the work of the best traders I know. Their success is directly linked to their degree of preparation for the trading day. Whether you do this work yourself or create a team of people to do it, there is no way around this kind of digging which, in time, will reward you richly. While I do not propose to offer a complete guidebook to trading, this chapter is meant to convey the length and breadth of the task awaiting those who wish to trade in the zone.

What follows is included to impart some of the basic information you need to know to become an effective trader. Start with the basics and then work toward an interpretation of the information that is "out of the box" or beyond the scope of the average trader. With time and preparation, that level of thinking will lead you to the zone.

Finding Value in a Company

As we discussed in Chapter 5, to play this game to the maximum, you must do your homework. Part of that homework is understanding the dynamics of company evaluation so as to best determine whether to buy or sell a company.

"If you expand your knowledge base, it can change the game overnight," said one trader. "Take the retailing industry. What kind of analytics would you want to use or rely upon, or what kinds of inquiries would you make, to understand the significance of movements in the company so that your trading or investing would be more informed? To the extent that you understand the thought process, you can start doing your own analyses in companies with whom you are beginning to get involved."

You need more than one source of information about the company and more than one technique to value a company. You need to know sales, earnings, cash flow, assets, and management. You must be able to analyze fundamentals and news events, predict how companies will respond to events, and keep track of events. You should have information about share price and share price movements, some understanding of the balance sheet and income statement, and the ability to assess the quality of a company. Over time you should have some sense of:

Income Statement

- Revenues
- Gross, operating, and profit margins
- Earnings per share
- Cost of goods sold
- Depreciation
- Amortization

Cash Flow

- Cash flow
- Capital expenditure

Balance Sheet

- Receivables
- Inventories
- Shareholders' equity
- Assets
- Liabilities

Estimates

- Earnings
- Sales
- Margins

The most advanced traders try to assess companies and determine how things will evolve and even how Wall Street analysts may be upgrading or downgrading company prospects. "Group think never works," said Martin. "Information can be instantaneous or delayed. I want to be ready for Wall Street's response to company numbers, or new products, or basic reorganization issues, all of which may impact on the stock price. Even when the analyst knows something, he isn't allowed to confirm that he is upgrading a stock. The analyst's call and spin is the critical thing."

Of course, the master trader can also take advantage of opportunities when the analyst is not correct. When analysts make bad calls, there is sometimes an open door for the trader who is on top of his game.

The master trader pays attention to earnings announcements as well as the actions of the big "elephant" firms such as Morgan Stanley, Salomon Smith Barney, and Lehman, among others. He uses the order flow of the elephants to give him some indication as to how things are going.

A successful trader wants to know why an industry exists, the history of the industry, the major players, the drivers of growth in the industry, and the barriers to entry to the business. He wants to understand the business model, whether the business is scaleable, how to leverage the business model in order to understand whether a company is going to be profitable, and why one company will achieve greater profits and higher multiples than another.

The more you understand the business model, the more you can understand what it will take to make things work. The more you know, the better prepared you will be to talk to analysts about the companies they cover. However, beginning traders sometimes experience trepidation in these talks, fearing that they won't know enough to sound intelligent. To assist them, I asked one senior trader/analyst for a list of important questions to consider when talking to an analyst. A few of the more cogent questions he suggested were:

- What are the critical factors that make a stock attractive in this group?
- Are there seasonal trends in the stock's performance?
- Are there key number releases that can influence short-term price action in the stocks?

- What's the time frame of your recommendations?
- Which of your buys have a chance of working this month? Which are second-halfers?
- How long have you been recommending this stock?
- What is the history of the booms and busts in their group over the past few years?

If you can answer all these questions, then you are well on your way to being able to understanding the value of a company and how it may be trading in the market place.

"If you are going home with positions and own a stock overnight, you should know what is going on," said one trader "If something comes out that was public and anticipated, and you are unaware of it, it is irresponsible and stupid."

By taking a look at all your information and processing it into the "big picture" you can make more informed decisions about your trades. The analytical effort should be to distill things to their essence, not to be obfuscated by details. As one trader said: "This is less science and more art."

One way of keeping your information in focus is to talk to the companies themselves or visit their stores and factories in order to find inefficiencies or information discrepancies that can be translated into trades.

"I have to walk around the stores to understand the movement of the retail stocks," said Mario, another analyst/trader. "I have an analyst who spends his afternoon at large discount stores counting shopping carts. I have to do the same thing. It gives me a general idea of how the stocks are doing. I want to consider the mix of clothes merchandise, the way they sell it, the promotional activity, and inventory. If I walk by a major clothing store, and it is only offering khaki and cargo pants, the product mix is not good. If they are out of stock, it means they have a hot product. If they are out of the product and the distribution center is in California, and they have to order from Asia, it may impact the comps. If they have inventory, and the weather is hot for September, and their sweaters are stacked, and they have to mark down the sweaters, that will impact the margins. We have to visit companies and know what is going on. Just waiting for the Street to call us isn't enough."

Fundamental Reasons to Buy

What happens when you've gathered all the information you can find? How do you determine whether to buy? Of course, different variables are relevant in the analysis of different industries. For example, a positive analysis in retailing might make reference to such variables as:

- Good inventory controls, limiting markdown risk, and improving gross margins.
- Comp store sales above internal projections.
- Comfortable high-end of Street estimate and estimated expectations to beat them.
- Improved earnings that are about to be announced in addition to the fact that the chart patterns may be looking positive.
- If the stock is down year-to-date even though the fundamentals are good.
- Near-term catalysts (such as the company doing one-on-ones during a road show or a major fashion show that may have been well attended in the previous year).
- Reduced expenses.

Other positive catalysts may be reports of insider buying, a possible bid for a company, business tracking above plan, or the lifting of a convertible by arbitrageurs. However, if a stock has moved up because of rumors, it may make sense to wait for a pullback when impatient short-term money exits from the trade, if no announcement about the purchase occurs.

You can also expect a stock to go up if there is something like a company announcement about the addition of more outlets for its product or service or the conscious decision by the management to implement new strategies for additional growth. Again, whether it goes up will be influenced by the price of the stock. If it is already trading at very large multiples, these plans and expectations may not leave too much room for growth on the upside but, nevertheless, would still be considered positive for a company. Obviously, each situation must be weighed against the historical trends, how the competition is faring, and what is going on in the market, but these factors are worth considering whenever you can.

In addition, most companies in most sectors are likely to benefit from news that they are joining with a strategic partner or signing a reseller agreement to help sell their supply. They also usually benefit from news that a major brokerage house is projecting several years of solid growth or is initiating coverage of a stock for the first time. An additional bullish catalyst is when a company is on a "road show" and is guiding the Street to higher top line growth (i.e., telling the Street that they expect better results) and talking about new businesses. If traders believe that any of the new businesses have a chance of working out in the future, a stock is likely to trade more strongly. Buy when there are continued positive comments from the Street.

The technology sector, however, is more complex and requires some understanding of the complexity of these products and systems. Consider a software testing company. It may benefit from a huge Internet software buyout. An applications management software company may benefit from a transition from Internet infrastructure investment to managing those systems once they are installed. To trade these stocks successfully, you need to know the products and the interconnections between companies. It is also useful to know about the competition and the addition of procurement systems to product lines driving new sales momentum.

Let's look at another example—the oil sector. One positive for that sector would be advance notice that a company is having a significant upside surprise relative to the Street expectations of revenues because margins and price are coming through faster than expected in a given quarter. This type of news might also bode well not only for the company but its competitors, because oil companies in the OSX (Oil

Service Stock) index move as a group. Other factors that suggest companies are doing well would include beating estimates, an increase in "rig count," or a pickup in spending or in drilling.

Sometimes the trader will buy improving stocks on dips in combination with positive news information that has catalytic value, for example increased air fares, declining oil prices (and presumably lower costs), and better industry numbers overall. Again, all these things have to be weighed with all the other variables I have been talking about in this book.

Additional fundamental positives for taking a long position include:

- The fact that it is the end of a lockup (the period after an IPO when stock can't be sold).

- Management owns the majority of the stock or Wall Street analysts are putting out bullish pieces on a stock (to the extent that their pronouncements affect the perception of the value of the stock).

- The anticipation of a new deal that is going to increase the competitive value.

- When a company is buying back its own stock (5 percent or more of outstanding shares).

According to some analysts, another reason to go long on a stock is that it is undervalued relative to its history or to its group. But this is not always so. Sometimes historical valuation has an effect on current or future valuation, leading some companies to trade at discounts to their peers. These issues become more significant if added to other relevant variables, such as the fact that an upcoming analyst meeting is expected to be positive about news events.

For example, in pharmaceuticals you may have a story about new indications for a successful drug, a new marketing partner, announcement of a secondary offering of stock after a positive initial public offering (IPO), new approved products, or new drug delivery platforms or technology that may launch an entirely new strategic medical direction for a compound and a company. A letter of interest in one company may highlight the relatively cheap valuation levels of the company as compared to its competitors.

One caveat about taking long positions. Don't buy illiquid stocks until there is a catalyst such as a stock trading at a major discount to competitors, an upcoming report, or an upcoming split in a stock. Also, consider the valuation of the company. Ask the following questions:

- Wherc are shares currently trading?
- Is earnings per share (EPS) growth conservatively estimated?
- What is the longer-term EPS growth rate?
- In retail, what is the comp-store sales growth rate and expanding operating margin?
- What is the estimated stock price based on the continuation of the present multiple in the company?

A master trader needs to be able to read the flows as well as have the fundamental information. In determining whether to go long on a position, it is important to know how the stock trades over time in order to determine the ideal size of your position. The longer the time scale, the bigger the range you should trade in. You size your position based on the distance until you are wrong. If you thought the market would turn lower for a year, you would give it so much room on a monthly chart and so much on a daily basis. Decide how much room over how much time. Monthly, it might be 10,000 shares. On a daily basis you would give it 100,000 shares because the range is much smaller.

Case Study
A business that is transforming from an old company to a new company is a good example to consider for a positive buy. Let's consider LMN, a business-to-business (B2B) supply chain management solutions provider for information technology. This company was focused on a small- and medium-size business market, but transformed itself from an information technology equipment lease/sales company to a pure play e-commerce software

company. The company is eliminating its old economy business and focusing entirely on B2B. Positive catalysts include the fact that it has filed a "secondary" with a major brokerage house in the lead. The management "teach-in" has occurred and went well, and it is starting a road show. It will benefit from additional research coverage by the major brokerage house.

LMN has 1,500 customers with whom it has long-standing relationships and from whom it may be able to win B2B business. It sells at a substantial discount to competitors and a substantial discount to growth rate. It gains transaction in its space, has new senior management, and a superfat pipeline. It is a premier vendor partner of other companies like Oracle and Microsoft and is ready to let analysts start lifting numbers.

Other positives include:

- It has on-line sites that allow the company to increase on-line recruiting efforts and improve its ability to reach more customers through product education.
- It is undergoing mergers and acquisitions.
- Its stock is off its highs with no change in fundamentals and has underperformed its groups.
- It is hiring aggressively at the senior management level.
- Its billable hour per consultant is high.
- It has joint ventures with highly capitalized partners.
- It has an increased brand awareness.
- Internal strife has been quelled.
- Revenue visibility has increased.
- It has a new partner in the wings.
- It has gross margin improvement, improved refining margins, improved land drilling domestically, and natural gas exposure.
- Its sales force turnover has abated.
- Its stock has been upgraded.
- There is a company buyback of stocks.

All things considered, the sum of the parts indicates that this company could be valued higher. It is a good buy.

Successful traders understand how to use fundamental information in making trades. Where you are expecting that certain companies are having strong quarters and are doing well with their sequentials in the present quarter and that the guidance (i.e., the company projections given to the Street analysts about the company) for the subsequent quarters is likely to be the same, it makes sense to buy these stocks on a pullback in price so that you get the best possible bang for your dollar. Where you are expecting an analyst meeting for a particular stock, you might also anticipate that the stock will move up into the meeting.

It also is worth paying attention to how a stock's competitors are doing. There may be a huge valuation gap between one company and its competitor, but the company may have an interesting story, may be having a good quarter, and may be expected to pick up in value until it is priced similarly in the marketplace as its competitors, in terms of earnings per share and multiples, especially if a company is coming back strong in orders and is expected by analysts to do the high end of the range on revenues.

When a company is struggling because it is pulling in profits from the subsequent quarter, it has the highest gross margins, or it's struggling because of loss of divisions to others, it might be a good idea to sell the stock on a rally, especially if you think it will underperform in its group relative to its competition in the months ahead.

Just like a good shopper approaches a clearance sale with enthusiasm, savvy traders also get excited when they see these "red flags." They know there is the possibility of a profitable trade—a good deal. However, the wise shopper always checks those bargains for hidden flaws. As we mentioned before, the master trader looks not only at the variables that can be counted and measured, but also looks for the unseen factors as well.

Understanding the Unseen Variables

To trade in the zone, a trader must watch what people are doing and how they are reacting. Maybe the benchmark comes and the reaction isn't what he expected. He doesn't challenge the response. He reads the response as another type of information. He trades based on his belief but isn't wedded to his belief. He combines technical skills, emotional control, analytical skill, and intelligence. He considers all factors available, including those not immediately apparent, and then he takes action.

For example, what do you do when you get that gut feeling the market is going to crack? One thing to do is to use that feeling as an indication of how others are feeling, so you can position yourself relative to the action that is taking place and will take place in the market. Use your own experience to judge how others are reacting rather than just reacting to your own emotions. In effect your emotions are an indicator not only of your own experience but of the experiences of others. If you can use your emotions you will benefit from them and not be controlled by them.

"You want to have a sense of the perception of the world, how the world will treat the stock," said one trader. "Then you trade around that perception. You are looking for a divergence. For example, everyone is looking for a decline in interest rates. The stock hasn't moved. People don't want to get into it. They have been killed. Now you can set up for a good trade if interest rates go down."

See and hear what other traders are experiencing. Does it give you a clue as to what is happening in the market? Can you plan your trades with this insight in mind? If you work on it, you may soon get in touch with one of the most powerful tools used to get in the zone.

Case Study
"If I know a company well enough, I usually am able to predict the stocks reaction to a CEO's presentation at a conference, meeting with institutional investors, or related news events," said Joseph. "There are opportunities to make long bets or short sales before or after an event because of the initial emotional reaction to the situation, often made by less informed investors. For example, if I know that a very charismatic CEO of a company is going to be making a presentation to a large room full of investors at a tech conference who may not be as familiar with the story as I am, I can take advantage of this by establishing a position beforehand and

then booking my profits as they react to this 'charismatic' presentation. The fundamentals were still the same before and after the presentation, but I took advantage of the emotional response elicited by this presentation, selling into strength. Emotional trades, of course, are closely tied to fundamental and technical components, because only companies with solid fundamentals and technicals should be long candidates in front of these situations. But the reverse is also true. Sometimes these situations create great shorting opportunities, again due to the initial emotional response to a less sophisticated conference attendee or interpretation of a press release."

Not only can you use the emotional responses of others to signal a good trade, you can also use your own emotional response to help you in your trading. If you do so, you won't feel bad about your feelings. You will see them as physiological signals altering you in a powerful way and you will gain some objectivity in the face of the extreme emotional swings triggered by trading activity.

Trading in the zone requires that you be in touch with your feelings and that you use them as information, not as something to govern your trading. For example, a master trader may be fearful and bearish on Thursday, thinking, "This could be it." But if it isn't, he'll buy stocks. He positioned himself for a crash on Thursday, but he was also prepared for the 100-point bounce following the brief meltdown.

The master trader recognizes that the game he is playing is ephemeral. He knows the company but doesn't get caught up in its valuations. He will move in a minute. He'll buy other stocks, even though he came in expecting to be short. He has a view, but it doesn't get in the way of making money. He has a high tolerance for change, ambiguity, and new inputs. He is willing to say to himself, "Let the stock tell me. I will respond to the cues."

For example, DEF was an illiquid, volatile stock. Kyle shorted it and made 8 points in one day on 30,000 shares. "It was a tough stock. The spreads were $1.00 wide. It went up and down points," he said. "It was an $80 stock, a high beta stock. The company was trying to guide the Street lower in terms of earnings numbers. They were telling analysts to lower numbers because they were not going to earn as much as people expected. They went from a $1.00 to coming in at 80 cents. It was less of an earnings downside surprise. They had a responsibility to let people know. So, the analysts told the people the numbers would be less. It impacted on the price of the stock. The stock was down. The company wanted to manage the Street's perception of it."

The master trader understands this kind of image play. He focuses not only on the numbers and what is being said, but also on the *response* that is being given to the incremental information—how it is being processed. He does not value the company *solely* on the basis of earnings. He also considers the basis of predicted future earnings. He sees the commoditization of markets and the emotionality in the market. He realizes that you can't always *see* the value of a stock. On a daily basis, "value" may not even have a place. Over time, a company's ability to earn a rate of return in excess of the cost of total financing determines its level of "value."

This base of knowledge is necessary for you to begin the journey to the zone. This knowledge allows you to react better even though things are changing. It allows you to make predictions based on the movement in the markets. It allows you to move with the tide and understand what is going on. Is this a lot of information to gather, a lot of considerations to make? Yes. Is it worth it? Definitely.

Fundamentals are not self-evident. These are the basics, and you can't get away from them. To be a trader isn't that hard. To trade in the zone takes self-examination and work. Don't expect to reach mastery overnight. It takes a passion, and it takes a lot of time.

As one trader noted, "It takes a year of information to understand a company and what analysts are saying to be able to prepare for trigger events. Trading successfully takes work. It is not immediate gratification."

Part Three

Controlling the Risk

Chapter 7

Managing the Risk

Just because you're in a risky business doesn't mean you have to be a gambler. Indeed, many great traders are highly risk averse. They are always measuring risk and the probability of loss against the amount of pain they are willing to experience and the amount of profit they are seeking. They do this by a complex, highly intuitive process of monitoring their emotions, controlling their losses, and managing their capital in line with their performance, based largely on their experiences and success in committing to their results.

You, too, can learn to manage your risk. In order to get a handle on risk management, you need to ask yourself two questions:

1. How much risk can I tolerate psychologically?
2. Am I using my capital wisely so that I can continue to trade another day?

Basically, the best traders know when to get in and when to get out. They usually look for a 3:1 risk/reward ratio. The downside risk must be less than the upside potential. While there are several levels of success on the upside, there is only one level of risk on the downside. There are never multipliers on the downside.

Great traders decide on their exit points on the upside as well as the downside in advance of their trades. They establish an exit point based on the amount of profitability they want from a trade, taking into consideration commission and slippage costs. Then they get out of a trade before it reverses. They realize that when they get bigger and stay longer, they are increasing their risk, especially in highly volatile and illiquid markets. However, at times they also press the bet and add to their positions before the exit target is reached. But they are careful not to get too greedy.

In highly volatile markets, successful traders are particularly cautious in managing their positions. They are quick to adapt to changing circumstances and don't remain wedded to positions. They are continually moving stocks, mentally and physically, reviewing and renewing their choices.

For example, if a master trader is short and sees the market going down but his stock not coming in, he may start buying back the stock instead of waiting for the market to continue coming in. When he adds to a position, he considers how much additional risk and reward he is taking, knowing not to stretch his luck. When the position is going against him, he gets out at his exit point. The inability to get out of a long position can be a major problem for the emotional trader whose ego won't allow him to admit he's wrong in his stock picks or directional calls.

Successful traders get bigger in their winners and kick out their losers. They diversify when they get a chance to do so, recognizing that they lose the most money when they are too loaded up in one area of the market.

They evaluate each position on its own merits and never justify being in one stock by the fact that they are ahead in another stock. They are not always looking to recoup losses or to hit home runs. In fact, they are very clear about closing down their trading for the day once they reach a certain amount of loss.

"It's about making money. Ring the register. Take profits," said Chris. "Travel on trains that are moving. Make the better bets. Don't force trades that aren't there. Don't trade impulsively. Don't chum around with bad trades. Get out of losses."

As noted at the start of the chapter, your approach to risk management can be summed up by your answers to these two questions:

1. How much risk can you tolerate psychologically?
2. Are you using your capital wisely so that you can continue to trade another day?

You have to determine the range in which to trade and how much of your capital to risk on a trade. You must decide on a predetermined amount of capital you can lose so that if the market is going against you and you have reached your predetermined limit, you get out. That is disciplined, risk-managed trading.

Review Your Statistics

One way to help determine capital allocation and the risk/reward ratio that you should be considering is to review your statistics. Trading statistics can help profile various patterns of trading behavior and assist traders in maximizing their performance. The use of trade level data has made it possible to review performance statistics that can be used to identify specific and measurable patterns of trading behavior.

The data includes such things as the stock traded, the buy/sell indicator, the position initiation, liquidation indicator, price, quality and the like. Other information, for example, asset class, instrument (cash security, option, future, forward), market sector, volatility of instrument, beta or other benchmark correlation statistics, and average daily number, can be superimposed on the database. From these numbers, traders can infer:

- Profit and loss on individual transactions.
- Average transaction sizes.
- Average holding periods.
- Percent of transactions liquidating profitably.
- Average gains on winning transactions.

- Average losses on unprofitable transactions.

- Average profit by mode of execution.

- Average profit by broker or counterparty.

- Distribution of profit and loss (P&L) on long versus short trading ideas and across sectors.

In addition, the following daily time series regarding traders can be derived, including the P&L, size of the portfolio (measured in currencies or trade units), the number of trades, and the volatility index. Of course, a review of trading statistics can be beneficial for both risk managers as well as the traders themselves.

Beneficial for Risk Managers

By reviewing statistics, it becomes possible to run a trading account with greater regard for the amount of risk that traders are taking—making sure they are taking sufficient risk but not too much. Based on the expected results given the size of their capital allotment, risk managers can help ensure that traders have sufficient volatility in their portfolios to help them reach their targets.

When possible, I review trading statistics with the risk manager to see what traders have accomplished in the previous months, including their percentage of profitability and whether they are using their capital wisely. These statistics are useful in helping traders to adjust their trading behavior, control their losses better, and make alterations in their portfolios consistent with their objectives so that they have a better shot at reaching their goals and maybe even exceeding them.

Examining trading statistics gives you another kind of objectivity about yourself and is not about being right or wrong. Rather it is an attempt at making an objective assessment about the correct trading decisions to make going forward so as to give you more freedom and objectivity than you might have brought to your trading until now.

In effect, a review of performance statistics can help to:

- Determine strengths and weaknesses of traders.
- Determine the patterns of trading behavior that are repetitive and reflective of underlying beliefs and attitudes that impinge on trading.
- Provide limits and constraints to traders.

A review of statistics can help determine if a trader is overtrading in too many equities, scalping and trading too rapidly and missing opportunities, or trading too slowly and also missing opportunities to take profit. It can be determined whether the trader's losses are more excessive than his profits on a unit basis and whether he is gambling in a foolhardy way, if he is too "macho" about his trades, or whether he is reasonably cautious and trading sensibly in terms of good quality risk/reward balancing.

By reviewing statistics we were able to determine that one trader, Greg, was steadily getting better but that he wasn't using enough of his capital. Moreover, he wasn't holding his positions overnight and wasn't concentrating his efforts on a particular sector in which he could do more intensive work and preparation to increase his confidence in his trades.

Another trader, Ira, had $45 million of buying power and was up 78 percent but was only using a portion of the capital allocated to him. Therefore there was no reason to increase his buying power.

Jack, on the other hand, had $30 million in buying power. His annualized return was 34 percent. He was underperforming. His capital needed to be reduced.

Owen had been successful almost every day that he had been trading. He was up 187 percent with $15 million in buying power.

"This is hard core portfolio management," said Josh, an experienced risk manager at a large, successful hedge fund. "Traders have to trade within certain parameters. Generally what keeps people from playing the game is that they are not taking appropriate risk with sufficient size and volatility. They tend to be too balanced long and short, too diversified, and in too many names. We can drill down on that with diagnostics."

In effect, these statistical measures can be used for policy making and strategic planning at the enterprise level. They are useful, from a risk management viewpoint, to find the best possible ways of combining the performance of portfolio managers by way of reducing redundancies. When you are able to identify traders whose portfolios do not correlate, it is often possible to suggest capital allocation alternatives. Risk managers can use this data to redeploy capital in an effort to maximize the performance of those contributing the most profitability to the firm.

Beneficial for Behavior Modification

Whereas the risk manager is concerned with using transactions data to explain patterns of profitability and risk assumption in the actual trading patterns of the portfolio managers, the same data has value as well in understanding the psychological and behavioral dimensions of trading patterns in individual traders. An examination of traders' statistics helps to reveal certain characteristic patterns, which in turn helps to focus attention on behavior that can be modified The statistics help them to see things about their trading which are often not immediately apparent. Traders cannot argue with the statistics.

Of course, this strategy is not designed to change trading styles but to help traders increase their trading acumen by taking more risk. The performance analysis approach provides a mathematical basis or underpinning for helping the trader to stretch by determining how much he has to put on the books to reach his targets.

"The objective is to define patterns of repetitive behavior that can be identified and then modified," said Josh. "This data allows you to place big bets in those situations where you have an edge based on in-depth research and timing. This approach supports the idea of getting more aggressive with winners. It is a constant test of how your stocks react to earnings, announcements, catalysts (like conferences), and the macroenvironment that should allow you to get out of high-risk positions where you lack an edge."

By looking at the statistical characteristics of the portfolio for any persistent trading pattern that is positively or negatively correlated with profitability, you can identify underperforming accounts. That information can then be used to assist these traders in modifying their behavior to increase their profitability or limit their losses. If traders are taking too much risk, they can follow set exit points, trade less risky instruments and decrease the volatility of their portfolio, or stop using options. If they want to increase risk, they can add volatility to their portfolio, hold positions longer, or use options.

Traders generally believe they are trading because of the position and the movement of the stocks. But they actually bring a certain fixed behavioral response pattern to their trading and, try as they may to change, they cannot do so too readily because this response is imbedded in their behavioral patterns. Only by identifying these responses and then learning to look for critical variables that can be modified can they actually alter their behavior.

Of course, behavior modification is inherently difficult because of the discomfort factor associated with change and the tendency for people to prefer the familiar. But through the review of individual statistics, we can find a common ground to discuss specific, simple behavioral steps that traders can take in order to expedite changes in their trading practices.

Traders know that the numbers don't lie. Once pinpointed, the trader can be guided to change particular bits of behavior quite independently of the specific trades she is making. She can learn to break boundaries by setting up new targets and learning new trading behaviors. Let's look at another example of this kind of assessment here.

Case Study
Victor is an experienced trader who 10 years ago learned to scalp and take quick profits. Victor was predisposed toward the bearish side of the market and for the past 8 years had been waiting for the market to turn down. A review of his statistics revealed that his P&L was negatively correlated with his average holding period, suggesting that he was practicing less than optimal liquidation techniques. His statistics showed this tendency to scalp and get out too fast. He had considerable difficulty holding on to winners. His holding period of trades averaged out to about 3 hours. This period was among the shortest holding periods for traders in the firm and quite consistent with Victor's sense of himself as being "an old tape trader."

His difficulty in holding on to winners was also demonstrated by his extremely low level of profits taken on winning shares (0.35 cents). Further demonstrating the scalping nature of his account and the fact that he was extremely good at getting in and out of many shares and stocks and still maintaining a profitable year was the fact that the number of his trades was extremely high. Thus, he was working very hard to make his money when he could have been more profitable with fewer trades and transactions.

In addition, his average win per share was .35, and his average loss per share was .33, giving him a win/loss ratio of 1.06. His losing positions were not sizable, but his winning positions were not as large as they could have been.

When Victor addressed these issues, he consciously lengthened his holding period and was able to increase the size of his profits, the size of his position, and his average winning profit per trade. Over the years, his trading produced an extremely high risk-adjusted return. The statistics pointed to the fact that he made his money through a high winning percentage (55.16 percent). Victor was extremely effective in selecting stocks and had an uncanny ability to read the moves of the marketplace.

Victor's problems were the result of what he himself characterized as "impatience and immaturity." For the past 8 years, awaiting a market downturn, he had been very fearful that the bull market had been about to end. As a result, he was very uncomfortable about holding on to stocks for any length of time and lost considerable opportunity when stocks that he had shrewdly selected kept going up, long after he had taken his small profit.

Victor was able to anticipate stock moves well in advance of the curve but lacked the confidence to play his insights. Having dramatically identified this pattern, I was then in a position to teach him a number of relaxation and meditative techniques. In this way he could reduce the internal pressure on himself to trade rapidly out of positions, gain confidence in his stock selection ability, and increase his profitability by at least doubling his usual time of holding. Much emphasis again was placed on encouraging him to stay longer in his positions so that as his holding period increased, his winning size per share would increase, and his ratio of wins/losses would improve.

By extending his holding periods, Victor made considerable progress, but the size of his positions and the amount of his capital used changed very little. Over time it became apparent that he was also a perfectionist who focused a lot of energy and emotionality on his losses and spent a good part of the day chasing his tail, trying to catch up, afraid to pay up for a position that he missed. The psychological severity of losing was greater than the excitement of winning. Overall, he handled far more stocks (20) than he could reasonably handle. Eventually, as he became aware of these issues, he did more preparation, traded fewer positions, and learned to stick to his convictions and hold his positions longer.

He focused much attention on expanding his holding period. By September 1998, he was up $600,000, a record for him in one month's trading. He was still trying successfully to be conscious of the need to extend his time frame from 3 hours a day to 6 hours or longer. As long as he holds his positions for longer time periods, he is able to trade bigger and show more profitability in his winning trades.

Victor still needs to get into larger positions to start with, especially in big money names. Unfortunately, he continues to spread his energy and insight out too far and does not maximize profitability in the biggest and best trades. For example, he noticed that instead of getting bigger in U. S. Steel and maximizing his profitability, he was getting into a couple of $5 and $7 steel stocks. Victor is cognizant of this problem and is trying to play bigger in the bigger names where the moves are greater. He has to put himself into the positions he believes in rather than cautiously avoiding involvement by doing busy trading but not strategic trading.

With the addition of research and insights gleaned at conferences, Victor began finding a way to increase his confidence and overcome his perfectionism. He was at least willing to admit that his winning percentage of 55 percent suggests that he can pick stocks, but that his average profit per winning trade was still too low suggesting that he was playing like an "amateur."

"I have a problem when the market is not telling me whether I am wrong or right," Victor noted. "I stick with a trade until I am proven wrong by price. This may keep me locked into one trade."

By September 1998 Victor was not getting attached to his market commentary and was learning to be light-footed and able to take profit. He was consistently having $60,000 days, in far contrast to the past. By November, Victor was starting to do more work. He began to keep a journal of recommended trades and their outcomes. He started to look for company-specific information that would move a stock in a short time frame.

By reviewing statistics in this way, trading managers and coaches and traders themselves can identify many such trading patterns that negatively affect performance. Then traders can be taught and encouraged to hold their good positions longer and to get out of their losing positions more rapidly. Statistical review is another aspect of trading which can, like gaining information, help confirm and enhance a trader's conviction and therefore, his ability to trade in the zone.

Play Bigger

The biggest obstacle to great success is the reluctance to add when it is right. To be as successful as possible, traders must play bigger, but this action does not come without discomfort or risk.

To simply get bigger and not improve the quality of your trades makes you subject to a major event. If you are putting together good ideas in terms of winning percentages, you have to improve the quality of your trades. The risk of increasing your size is that if something happens, you can blow up. If you improve the win/loss ratio, hold it longer, and get out of losses, you can lessen that risk.

When seeking to play bigger, there are certain characteristics of stocks to consider. Look for stocks that are liquid, where there are catalysts, and you have good risk/reward probabilities. Make sure you can get out of the position, especially when you are trading short.

If you are in the stock for a reason, you shouldn't sell it just because it is down. If it goes down because of the market action for the day, trade around the position and buy more. However, you should also know at what point you should take the loss. Again, develop a strategy with defined entries and exits. Then trade your strategy.

"We need to be in stocks for a reason," said one trader. "Unless the reason changes, we need to stay in them."

If 3 percent to 10 percent of your trades accounts for 100 percent of your profitability, then the key is to let profits run and cut your losses. In other words, get bigger when you are winning.

"Your performance is not in your bad bets but in not making enough in good bets," said Mark. "You have to keep losses down. That is automatic. You know when you have lost money and where you made $3 million when you could have made $20 million. The big thing is to focus on ones where you were right but complacent. You have to make sure you are not sitting on trades that could be part of that small percentage of profitability."

Getting bigger is a form of intuition based on intelligence and open-mindedness. The master trader must have a highly deterministic ability to distill things down accurately and not be so committed to his data that he can't accept when he is wrong.

"In the thick of the battle I sometimes make poor decisions," said Sam. "I might kick a good idea out because it is not working at the time. I need to increase my holding period and find solid ideas that I can live with when the S&Ps [Standard & Poor's] go down 30 points and there are no bids for them. If the market changes direction or starts to go against you and you still have the reason (which will give you confidence), then you should stay with the stock."

Traders need to understand volatility, have a core portfolio, and hold longer. There is a range where volatility makes sense and a range where you lose control. If you have a rough stretch, cut your risk. If you are uncertain, it is OK to sell some or all of your stock. But remember, if you reenter later when there is more certainty, up the ante and don't fret over entering at a higher price. Sometimes that is the cost of making a confident decision instead of an emotional one.

Case Study

Travis was afraid of taking losses and, as a result, often scalped his stocks rather than getting bigger and holding them longer.

"I should add when it is right," he said. "I have to use more capital. My average capital usage has been $5–10 million. For the year it was $12 million. The goal is to get it higher. When I know it is right, I am not maximizing the position."

Travis needed to look at the volatility of his portfolio and not how many dollars he was working with. He was in low volatility names. He shouldn't have put on trades just to use capital. He needed to increase the volatility of his trades.

To make more profit, a trader needs higher volatility. A master trader makes a concerted effort to size things, to look for things that may germinate over time. Travis was unconsciously putting on hedges so that his overall P&L volatility didn't increase. What could he do to improve on that?

"Have a couple of value plays," I suggested. "Look for things that may take several weeks. Trade around them. Trade some futures to enhance your viewpoint and as a hedge. Of course, when you go home down 400,000 two or three days in a row, you can't feel the world is coming to an end. It's not easy, but a little pain is what it takes to make a lot of money."

As one trader said, "You need to take pain to go to the next level. The daily fluctuations have to be higher. That is the goal to work on."

Although traders may make money without significant losses, to get to a bigger range, losses are inevitable. More volatility leads to more losses but also bigger wins.

We admire Michael Jordan and other star athletes because of their capacity to remain in a state of equanimity despite extraordinary success. As much as it increases their confidence, they set higher and higher goals so that they work harder. Traders should also set the bar higher.

As long as you do the work, you can get bigger. However, when traders start to think they have a special ability rather than understanding that it is the work they have done, they are heading for trouble.

Integrate your success into your sense of self so as to revisit it on an as-needed basis. Acknowledge your good experiences so that you can gain confidence, but then work harder by setting more challenging goals.

Case Study
Christopher is another trader who was not utilizing his natural ability. He needed to play bigger on the S&Ps and trust his intuition more. In his shorts, where he had been right, he had basically been too small and not trusted his instincts. He needed to examine the broken companies and short more when the stock was going up. He was being too cautious and was not going short enough to make big money.

"I am making $70,000 in profits, but I have three longs that cost me $70,000 every day," he said. "I still have a net loss of 50 grand. I could have been short. I could have focused on broken situations. I had a sense the market would go down and come back up. I learned that in a busted situation you have to take some pain and short more when you are right. I thought I was big, but I wasn't big enough. I was short but not short enough."

Master traders see each day as a new day. They don't worry about yesterday's profit and loss, or tomorrow's. They are only concerned about what they are doing today. Beginning traders often find it easier to just take the profit. What they miss is the challenge of grappling with new concepts and the confidence that comes with playing bigger and earning.

"I want them to manage their profit and loss volatility," said one trading manager. "They need to think not in terms of units or shares or amount of capital. I want them to think in terms of volatility. How much is a given position going to cause your P&L to fluctuate daily? You have to know the volatility of the portfolio, not every stock."

Case Study
Matthew has been trading for a year and is finally making some headway. He has picked a group to focus on and is working with a senior trader as his mentor.

"I am trading size," said Matthew. "Last month I did $400,000. Now I am moving out to another level, but I don't want my expectations to get too high. If I expect to do this every month and then I don't, I may get disappointed."

If Matthew maintains the same discipline, he should continue to succeed. He needs to keep looking for the ones that are moving and play the size he is playing. To continue his success, Matthew needs to continue to extract generalizations from what he is doing and watch how he is responding to the market.

"Once you break through, you will never go back," said one master trader. "Whatever you were afraid of, you will have mastered. Hopefully, you will then have the discipline to keep playing the new game."

Matthew increased his goal from $1.5 million this year to $5 million next year. "One year ago I was nervous about 2,000 shares," he said. "Now I can move to 100,000 shares for next year. It all depends on whether you are willing to step up to the plate."

Risk management is crucial for a trader to be in the zone. It is critical to cut down on losses and take profits in winning trades. To do so means moving capital from losing trades to other potentially profitable situations where you can take advantage of the intraday volatility. This type of trading requires flexibility, a willingness to take shorter-term profits, and to follow one's predetermined strategy. At the same time, traders must maintain a core position to add to when there is a dip in price and in order to benefit from the maximum long-term gain in the stock. In this way, traders manage their pain and maintain enough capital to continue trading tomorrow.

Building a Portfolio

When considering risk management, each trader needs to consider his objectives, his strategy, and the risk parameters involved. The same basic questions and parameters must be assessed and then adjusted according to the basic assumption of the asset class you are trading. The following list of considerations were suggested by Paul, an experienced manager who runs a balanced "book"—where the dollar value of long-term positions approximates the dollar value of short positions in the portfolio:

- What is your monthly objective? Consider what your book or portfolio should look like to produce that result.
- What percentage of your capital is allocated to high conviction bets? A reasonable percentage would be 75 percent distributed among 10 or 12 stocks.
- What is the price at which you will add to the position?
- What is the price objective for the trade?
- What is the downside risk—the price at which you will stop yourself out of the trade?
- What is the risk/reward ratio?
- What degree of confidence do you have in your risk parameters?
- What do the fundamentals say about the values you have chosen?
- What work have you done to support your choice? Have you talked to more than one analyst?
- What is your level of conviction about the trade independent of the risk/reward measure?
- Does the risk/reward of your big bets look better or worse than your little bets?
- What do the technicals suggest about the movement of the stock?
- Are there any catalysts that you are waiting for?
- Is your portfolio balanced between long and short bets?
- How fast can you get out of your low conviction bets?
- Can you reduce low conviction bets to 25 percent of your portfolio?

Case Study
Based on his answers to these questions, Paul began to consider what a $5 million portfolio should look like. He then began to create a business model based on performance, where capital was regularly being reallocated to the most profitable ideas. For Paul, a key was to keep moving capital from dormant to active stocks.

"If you make a little money every day, psychologically it primes you to make the big bets," he said. " I learned early on to press bets. Success begets success. Make your bet sizes bigger. Always keep considering what percentage of your capital is in your big bets."

Paul and his partner, Randy, developed a strategy that combined a short-term, catalyst-driven approach capturing the intraday volatility of stocks with a long-term, valuation-based analytical approach. This strategy created a portfolio designed to deliver more profitability by running both an active short-term book versus a long-term buy/hold portfolio. It's a mixed tactic, combining high turnover with long-term bets. Their portfolio takes advantage of fundamentals, short-term catalysts, and awareness of the price action or supply demand characteristics of the market as manifested in the tape action. Having chosen to have 75 percent of their capital in their biggest bets, they decided to clean up some not-so-strong bets in less favorable positions where they lacked conviction.

"When we are right, we have to play big," said Paul. "We also have to cut our mistakes faster. We have to react quickly to being wrong. It's the magnitude of the mistakes that make the most difference in our profit and loss."

Paul and Randy worked out a number of pragmatic trading principles to help implement this kind of risk management strategy. Their basic plan was as follows:

- The bulk of money should be in high-confidence trades. Get out of a stock that isn't moving or that has already had its move and where there is no imminent catalyst, news event, or earnings announcement that is likely to move the stock. Put the capital to better use in stocks that have a better chance of moving.

- Keep looking for the right ideas and replace good ideas with better ones (more active trades with intraday volatility).

- Keep adding to the winning positions and keep reducing or eliminating the size of losing positions, unless there is a reason to suspect that by buying the dips you are preparing for more profitability on the upside.

Paul and Randy are constantly reassessing their positions. As the market discounts the positive earnings, their positions on the stock can move from positive to negative. For example, they were short a large-cap cyclical company in the summer of 1999. The fundamental earnings for the second quarter of 1999 had already been factored into the price. Logically, positive earnings were positive for the stock, but in this case the good news was reflected by the recent strength. Therefore, it was essential to weigh the earnings in the context of recent stock movement, company fundamentals, and the outlook going forward.

"My basic philosophy was always to replace good ideas with better ideas at the end of a longer time period," said Paul. "Now I realize I can substitute stocks on a much shorter time frame. It may be a good three-month idea, but I can ask myself what is good for today? One of these ideas can make five points in a day and then ten more points. I need replacement ideas. In fact I need more ideas than money."

"I want to participate in the daily volatility," he continued. This is where you improve and make the money. We have to move our feet. We can't be inflexible. Don't take losses just because you are longer term. Have your capital constantly working."

To manage risk and allocate capital most efficiently, traders need to be aware of the catalysts, such as earnings, the fundamentals, and the price action or supply and demand character of the stock. These variables are especially important for the equity trader. Using this information, the intelligent trader does a probability analysis of the risk/reward of a trade before he gets into it.

Remember, the market is a natural laboratory for studying risk-taking behavior. The trader's decision-making capability is put to the test in this highly volatile and unpredictable environment. Risk management is, therefore, an essential weapon in the arsenal of the master trader and a vital link to trading in the zone.

Chapter 8

Tolerating the Pain

Negative feelings, anxiety, discomfort—all these emotions sometimes go hand in hand with risk. But they can be managed and ultimately, mastered.

In Chapter 7, we examined some of the financial dimensions of risk, in particular calculating how much risk you can afford so that when things don't turn out favorably you are still able to trade another day. Now, let's explore a more subtle dimension of risk—the psychological dimension. We will look specifically at the amount of "pain" you can tolerate as you take on varying degrees of risk commensurate with the potential profits you seek.

The market exacerbates a range of emotions, including fear, greed, pride, frustration, and panic. Indeed when there is uncertainty and the market is choppy, you can often see that emotion is moving the market. As one trader observed: "Selling leads to more selling as everybody jumps off, and buying leads to a return of optimism and more buying. There is no certainty. Everyone follows the crowd."

Master traders judge their success in large part by their adherence to their strategy in the face of wide and unpredictable oscillations in the market, not simply by their profit and loss. This means staying disciplined and managing their emotions so that they can adhere to their strategy in the face of all kinds of pressure to abandon it.

Control Your Emotions

Much of my work with traders has involved helping them to understand and master their psychological responses to the market so that they can trade more successfully without being distracted by their own emotional responses. Indeed you can learn to keep your risk under control by managing your emotions, along with your reactions to your emotions, and by separating your own negativity and competitiveness from the objective assessment of a stock.

Although it is difficult to manage or control the environment, you can learn to trade in the zone, focusing on the important issues at hand and ignoring both external and internal distractions. Just as actors in a workshop learn to work and express on cue a range of painful emotional experiences that most of us tend to avoid or suppress, you can learn to manage or ride out the wide range of feelings experienced during the course of trading that can throw you off your strategy and reduce your ability to handle risk. You can learn to experience these feelings without overreacting to them.

All of us are subject to mind traps. We respond to ostensibly neutral events with habitual responses from the past. We react to events and our physiological and emotional responses to them through the filter of our own emotional reactivity, which leads in turn to automatic responses such as fight or flight and some justification or rationalization of our responses. Because this response is automatic we keep responding the same way to events so that the world keeps looking the same way to us day in and day out, year in and year out. This reaction happens everywhere, especially on the trading desk in highly volatile and unpredictable markets.

Nevertheless, traders can learn to separate all stimuli or trading events from their own automatic responses and interpretations so that they can respond to trading events in new ways related to newly defined and creative trading objectives. In response to any negative stimulus or event, the first step is to consider exactly what happened. Ask yourself the following questions:

- What are the facts?

- What was the specific event that triggered your emotional response?

- What bodily sensations did you feel?

- What emotions did you feel?

- What meaning or interpretation did you give to the events, for example, "I'm dead. My stock just cratered."

- What was your decision in the moment of reactivity? Did you decide to hold on to a dropping stock because of fear, hoping against hope that it would turn? Did you hold on to a winning stock instead of taking your profit because of greed or the feeling that maybe you could make a killing?

- What benefit did you derive from your reaction? Did it, for example, allow you to blame the markets or bad luck for how the trade worked out, or did you use it to beat yourself and bemoan your stupidity? These are excuses that may have kept you from taking full responsibility for figuring out what work had to be done to make the trade more successful.

- Is this response typical for you?

- Could this response be linked somehow to a life principle of yours?

- What alternative responses might you have made in the situation?

- How much more flexible could you be if you could stay calm and stick with your original strategy or rethink the meaning of new data in a nonreactive way?

Remember, in most instances it is not the events themselves that account for why you feel the way you do. You don't usually become anxious because of a specific event. Rather you become anxious because of your habitual interpretations of the event, and in a busy trading day these interpretations can be happening all the time.

As you review negative or failed trades and separate fact from interpretation and emotion, you will gain new insight into your trading.

When you can distinguish the facts as facts, you will be able to create new structures for dealing with events themselves rather than being compelled to act in terms of your interpretation. You will no longer have to do all kinds of irrational and emotionally loaded things to reduce your anxiety.

Case Study
Zack, an experienced manager of a medium-sized hedge fund, would often get stopped out of a position by small shifts in the opposite direction until he learned to ride out his anxiety and not let it color his interpretation of market movements.

"One of the best ways to manage your emotions," I told him "is to time them. Use a stopwatch to time the actual experience. Take note of how long your feelings last. Keep a notebook of your feelings and record your thoughts for as long as they persist."

"As you do this, you will begin to notice a certain phenomenon. The next time you feel that way again, you will have a frame of reference for the experience and will find that the feelings are less intense and last a much shorter amount of time. At a certain time when you are experiencing the feelings, but not trying to get rid of them, the feelings will fade. You will not be able to create them no matter what mental image you conjure up. Eventually, you will have mastered the feelings and will not experience the pain of them. You will have taken ownership of the feelings. This will give you enormous flexibility in your trading so that you are not run by your own emotional reactivity."

Zack practiced this tactic for several weeks, and each week he reported a greater capacity to handle his feelings. After four weeks it was no longer an issue, and he wasn't being spooked out of his trades by "market noise."

There is no way to eliminate negative feelings. To trade in the zone, you simply have to learn to ride those feelings out. Instead of trying to get rid of your emotions, embrace them, measure them, and learn about them. The traders who have learned to trade in the zone have confronted their own fears and recognized them as part of being involved in the activity of trading.

Fear

The uncertain and chaotic nature of the markets helps to foster anxiety, uncertainty, and fear. Trading in the realm of uncertainty typically triggers insecurity because you don't know which way things are going to go. This reaction is normal, but insecurity triggers anxiety, which in turn can lead to panic, paralysis, overreaction, and a variety of emotionally crippling states of mind. These states of mind can produce major trading mistakes such as not getting big enough in winning positions, covering short positions too soon, failing to move into more opportunistic trades, or failing to allow yourself to ride out such events as a short squeeze.

Fear throws you off your game. You can't concentrate on assessing reality when you are in that kind of a reactive state. When you become aware of how you are reacting and how you are trading on the basis of your reaction, you can correct for it and see reality a little bit more clearly.

The secret to trading in the zone is to be able to face reality, to know yourself, and to apply yourself to your objectives. You must learn to recognize fear and sometimes be able to do the thing you most fear. As you face your fears, you let yourself see your own hesitation so that slowly you can enter into the realm of the fear. Notice and perhaps keep a written record of the physiological components of anxiety such as palpitations, dizziness, shortness of breath, muscle tension, sweating, chest pain, nausea, dizziness, numbness or tingling, restlessness or being easily fatigued, difficulty concentrating, and irritability.

It is especially useful to time the duration of your responses, as I encouraged Zack to do. Timing frames the experience for you and gives you some assurance that such an experience will not last forever. To your amazement, you soon discover that an extended reaction, which seemed to last forever, soon becomes encapsulated into a few brief moments so that as you allow yourself to experience the fear, it dissipates rapidly and turns into energy.

Timing your responses helps you to recognize when you are having difficulty and how your anxious thoughts are linked to your results. Spend time trying to understand the relationship between your thoughts and your results and you will discover that you have control over your thoughts and your actions and can bring them in line with your intended results.

When data supports your fears, you can use the facts to make rational choices. However, if your trading is governed by fear, your flexibility and capacity to handle your risk is limited, and you become the victim of reactive decisions made under the influence of strong emotions.

More often than not, traders are influenced to make bad risk management decisions because of fear. If you are making the choice because you are afraid, then you are not trading in the zone. For example, there is frequently a denial of reality and fearful signals at the beginning of a trade. If the trader becomes overly conscious of this fear, he allows himself to become terrified and panicked, then he may sell too soon.

You need to be aware of your fear early on and then manage it well. You don't want to eliminate fear. You want to use it. Fear is not entirely bad. It can alert you to pending problems in the market and can help you to recognize what other traders are feeling and perhaps doing reactively. If you can master your own fearful feelings, you can take advantage of this built in early warning system and trade counterintuitively against the crowd. When you use your fear as an indicator, you are trading in the zone.

Pride

When you are trading in the zone, you do not let ego or pride get in the way. You are not attached to your opinions or ideas and are willing to change your positions as the market dictates. You can sell something you have just decided to buy and vice versa without worrying that you seem to be inconsistent. You are constantly tweaking your positions to maximize profitability. If you are wrong, you acknowledge it and move on. You are not bound to hold on to an idea or check with someone else when you change your mind.

You also are not attached to the ways in which you trade your positions. You are not looking for home runs but just to hit the fat part of the pitch. You do not trade like some traders who avoid certain trades because they are mundane or commonplace rather than creative or original. You care little for trying to be brilliant. As such you won't let pride can get in the way of trading in the zone by deciding that second best is simply not good enough. Unlike traders who are run by their egos, you won't bypass trades that will make money because you think that you are getting in too late to get the maximum benefit.

One especially smart trader who took great pride in his intellect told me: "Trading to make money seems to be an idea that points to doing less than I can. I don't trade unless I can do my best. I say to myself, 'This is going to work, but I could have bought it cheaper.' Then I overcompensate and plow into it excessively—overtrading. I am too affected by my thoughts about the way I *should* be trading and it interferes with my actual trading."

Traders who are too caught up in their opinions about their ideas and are stuck on their own in-depth analyses often cannot get in the moment. They are not trading in terms of their goal or strategy but in terms of their pride. And pride can cost them a lot of money if it makes them miss opportunities for success and keeps them from trading in the zone.

Panic and Depression

Often irrational things happen in the market that cause traders to panic. When you are trading in the zone, you are able to sense when something is going on that is the product of panic. You can harness your emotions and remember the rational reasons for buying your stocks. You are grounded by your knowledge of the fundamentals of the companies you own and technical assessments of your positions and can ride out swings in the marketplace that temporarily may be affecting your stocks. At the same time, you pay close attention to the price action, which tells you something about the supply and demand of a stock and the psychology of the trade and helps you to make decisions to reduce or expand the size of your positions.

Case Study

On one day in the summer of '99, the bid offer in one consumer product stock was 102½ to 103. It remained there for a while. Buyers kept stepping in at 103 until the sellers were cleaned out and the supply lifted. Buyers then had to pay up until finally the stock went to 112.

While this tug of war was going on between buyers and sellers, Lenny saw the volume go up in a big way and became interested. He bought 70,000 shares. Then he noted that a lot of short sellers were getting involved and he became concerned that the stock might go back down to 99 if it broke through 103. He started doubting his own conviction and became reluctant to buy more stock.

"I stayed in there and took all the pain of uncertainty. I also spoke to my analyst who had some doubts because of some news, and that shook me up. I started to panic and sold half my position and made $2 or $70,000 on 35,000 shares. It could have been a half million dollar trade if I had held on to the position and not panicked."

What Lenny is talking about is panic on the basis of some bad news that prompted him and other traders to sell. Their selling started a selling rally until those who were long in the stock couldn't tolerate the pain of losing, capitulated to the panic, and got out of the stock. When everyone was out of the stock, buyers started bidding again and began moving the price up.

"If I had stayed in a little longer or gotten bigger, I would have made more money in that position," he said. "I was holding for earnings. I knew the number. I really knew it. For some reason there was a lot of chatter in the market that there would be a bad number that created panic. I knew the chatter was wrong, but I got caught up in it. I should have taken advantage of it."

When you are trading in the zone you are able to take the pain of waiting for something to unfold and able to experience the tension of the trade. You can understand what factors affect other traders and what is influencing the price action of a stock. The important thing is that you can follow companies and not be taken out of your strategy by market fluctuations.

Case Study
Another trader, Ben, explained how panic holds him back: "I am able to pull the trigger, but then I get scared and cannot stay with

a position. It's a physical feeling. My heart is going fast. I am short of breath and fearful. I think I will be fired. My thoughts are racing. I have no problem getting into the position. I just want to get out of the position. It's gotten worse and worse. If I were in the safest stock in the world, the way I am feeling, I couldn't trade it. My execution is poor because of the panic. I am overtrading. I get panicky and head for the exits."

A closer examination of this trader showed that part of his panic resulted from being unprepared. He had spent too little time getting the information he needed.

"I pick up the phone 50 percent of the time when 2 percent of the calls are for me. I feel compelled to help people with their computers. I listen to people I don't want to listen to. I look at their trades. I put too much weight on their judgment. No one knows more about my trades than I do. I am picking up anxiety from other traders. I pick up the mood in the room. I tell everyone what I am trading. I hate being asked what I am doing and how I am doing. I should be trading my own opinions."

Ben has a sense of obligation to share his views, to explain what he is doing, one of the main factors leading to his panic and subsequent depression. In order to begin trading in the zone, Ben has to see what he is doing to burden himself. By telling people about his trades, he locks himself in. He feels he then can't get of his positions because he is waiting for others to trade their position before he does what he wants. All of these factors are contributing to such an emotional overload that he has no energy left to concentrate on his trading goal.

This trader is trapping himself in a box, which limits his flexibility and the freedom he has to trade. It further burdens him and produces the panic.

For Ben to reduce the panic, he needs to take some of the unnecessary pressure off himself and extend his time horizon. He needs to relax into the trade and remember how successful he has been in the past. He needs to stop seeking reassurance. Again, the key is to have a plan and to implement the plan, not to trade on the basis of your emotions.

Handle the Losses

A crucial part of risk management is the ability to handle losses. The best traders are willing to take risks without any certainty of the outcome. They have confidence in their methods. However, if a master trader loses, he does not wait until his confidence returns before he starts trading again. He is not relaxed about his losses, but he makes the conscious choice to get out of a losing mind-set. He chooses to be positive and to start looking for new opportunities. He won't let himself get caught up in his reactions to loss. He doesn't spend too much time in self-rejection and self-criticism. Rather, he notices his loss and gets back to playing the game. He knows that confidence is the product of performance not a precursor of it.

The master trader finds no virtue in being preoccupied with the loss or beating himself unnecessarily. He doesn't have to be right most of the time. He only has to make more profits in his winning trades than he loses in his losing trades.

One well-known trader didn't make money for a year and a half. He suffered from big swings but kept on betting. He started trading with smaller bets and then he came roaring back, proving that confidence comes from getting into the game.

"You get so low that you believe you have nothing more to lose and so you get back in. The ground is so solid that you have nowhere to go but up," he said. "In my heart I wanted to play, but I wasn't filtering it through the necessity of making money everyday. Making money on a daily basis is the highest form of what we do. It is not pedestrian at all. It involves commitment. It is about focus. You have to do it that way."

The problem with loss is that it can set in motion a variety of maladaptive responses with negative consequences for subsequent trades. The emotional trader, seeking to recoup his losses, may begin to flail about and expose himself to even riskier trades, rather than stemming the tide by controlling his downside risks. He may hold on to losing positions far longer than makes sense, hoping against hope that his failing positions will rally. In all of this he risks losing more of his confidence as well as opportunities to make gains by better allocation of his capital.

"The problem with holding on to losing trades," explained Eugene, "is that it complicates matters for you. For one, it may lead to a greater loss if the stock you are holding on to keeps going down. It may also lead to missed opportunities. You may begin to get out of profitable positions elsewhere to compensate for your loss. When you hold on to losing trades you tie up your capital (and attention), which could be earning more money elsewhere. On top of all this it may have a negative effect on your psyche."

Far too often when positions reverse, traders also get emotionally whipsawed and compulsively seek a quick profit as things improve. They hesitate to hold on to winning positions because they are anxious to avoid the trap of falling stocks again. At this point emotion—rather than reason—governs the upside of their trades.

Case Study
Derek lost the focus of his target when he lost money. He got hurt, backed off, and couldn't get back in his game. He needed to get back into the rhythm and not focus on the loss. Instead, he concentrated on how to eliminate losing.

Derek didn't understand that losing is part of the game. He has to be able to take those hits if he wants to make his profitability target of $8 million a year. I told him, "Your average P&L [profit and loss] swings are on the order of $100,000 a day—winning and losing. Based on your performance that will make you $300 to $400,000 a month but won't get you to $8 million. If you doubled your size, and your risk-adjusted performance dropped, you could do it. But the biggest hurdle will be negative $200,000 three or four days a month. You have to rise above the losses. You need enough confidence to ride out the losses."

Just because a trader loses money doesn't mean that he didn't do something strategically sound for his portfolio. If the overall result is profitable, it doesn't matter that you lost money. Sometimes it may make sense to buy more as the stock goes down, if you believe it will eventually move upward. In select cases it is OK to stay in a losing trade or to buy more. It all depends on the analysis and not on the re-activation of hope, which may keep the trader in too long. That's why it's important to set a limit on your losses, but winning requires focusing on the target and not on losing.

"Manage your losses and ride your profits but not so much that you get caught," said one trader. "I want the losses to be low when we are wrong. When they work, I want to have four to five times the upside." The master trader can have a winning percentage of 30 percent but can make big money by managing his losing trades and riding his winning trades.

In addition to the uncertainty and the extreme volatility and liquidity of the markets, traders who are losing also have to contend with the psychological consequences of failure and in many instances newly discovered vulnerability. At some firms, where success is a part of the ethos, traders who are not making money have additional pressure put on them.

"If you go through a losing cycle here you feel like an odd ball. If it weren't for the fact that I made so much money for so many years, and I understood this so well, I'd be a basket case," said one trader.

Losing is definitely the piece of the trading game that is hardest to embrace. Success is usually easier even though it is often illusory. To get back in the game after a loss, traders have to start thinking about the target once more and must start building their positions commensurate with it. The virtue of the goal is that it tells you the level at which to play. It is a guideline for the future.

"Making money is the easy part," said Sandy, a master trader who doesn't allow ego to interfere with his strategy. "Losing money is the hard thing, but that is what keeps traders around. You have to develop the ability to cut losses. That is the tough part. That is what makes a trader good—managing losses."

It is important to continue to remember that generally only 3 percent to 10 percent of trades account for 100 percent of the profitability of most traders. Profit is concentrated in a limited number of trades, and the vast majority of trades are break-even propositions at best. In fact, at least 40 percent are losers. Again, the key is to minimize losses and maximize the winners.

One trader, Adam, had a particularly difficult year. He started well but ended up being flat. For him, the goal was to stay in the game when others were being forced out. He needed to remain confident and get past the natural tendency to resist stretching in the face of his losing year.

"I think about where I am. This is the worst year in five years for me. What is this going to do to me?" asked Adam. "How will I respond? How do I move on? I have thought about that a lot in the last few days. I am not pleased with where I am, but I know I have to go through this. I have to take losing more money until I right myself. This is a period of contemplation and inaction. I am trying to get at peace with it. That's all there is."

If you are behind, keep going for your basic daily goal, and don't try to recoup what you lost in a single day. The most important thing you can do is to keep your losses down and build a record of consistently being profitable. Doing so will build your confidence and help you prepare for the day when you can take bigger positions and make greater profitability. As one trader expressed it: "Traders are like kids. We want to win. We are sore losers. We are competitive guys who don't like to lose. When you are right, you feel on top of the world. When you are wrong, the pain is horrible and hard to live through, unless you know that a month from now it will be OK. When you have experienced the high, you can reference it to the low."

Control of the process is vital to the skill. More important than the transient exhilaration of the successful trade is the intellectual satisfaction of knowing how to do it. When you understand how to play, you can keep going when you are down. The pain and the euphoria are both just part of the process. If you are in the game you will have both. You understand the larger framework. You can ride out the pain by knowing there is exhilaration to come.

Case Study
Fred got whipsawed by the market the first week of the year 2000. He started to push the size and took a bigger drawdown than he was accustomed to. He got paralyzed by it and stopped playing his game of buying the dips. He lost his confidence and his concentration and stopped trading. This state of mind persisted into the second week of the year. On Monday, he started getting bigger

again, lost, and got panicky. He was really desperate to take a vacation and start over.

"I missed a number of massive opportunities," he said. "I can't get my head on right now. It scared me when I lost on Tuesday. It was a bigger, more violent loss than I was accustomed to. It was the wrong time to get big. The last few days have been horrific. I lost my conviction. Had I executed my plan, I would be up a million dollars right now. When I start to lose, it is debilitating. It is a mind game for me. I have good ideas. It just requires getting over the psychological hurdles."

Fred's scenario reveals something about the psychology of losing. A trader can be caught in a downward trading spiral which he must extricate himself from before he begins to win again.

"I had a loser mentality," said Fred. "I was getting out too soon. My gut gives me a high percentage of winning trades, but my execution is lousy. It's driving me nuts. I have to take a little bit of drawdown. I am not good at losing money. It affects me. I need more confidence. I keep thinking about my mistake."

"Here I am sitting on a potential gold mine, and I am squandering it," he continued. "I need to be more coherent. I have a good record. I must trust my instinct. If I had stayed with my strategy, I would have made a fortune. I stopped trading because I got scared. I ran out of energy."

Losses are natural and are supposed to look a certain way. Anxiety builds with each new day of losses. Therefore, it helps to know the duration of a drawdown. By knowing a little of what to expect, you can ride it out a little easier.

Day one through four, most traders can deal with it. Days five through eight, they start projecting their current situation into the future ad infinitum. Days nine and ten they are numb. By days eleven and twelve the cycle is over.

"Today is day ten," said Jeff. "At least now I know it is almost over. If I didn't know that, I would think it could go on forever. When people lose money they should keep track of how long their cycle is on the down side. What does a daily loss look like? What does a max peak to trough look like? When it happens don't act as if this is something new. This is the cycle you must go through on the way to increased size. You will lose more money because you are trading bigger size. If you can contain your feelings, you can ramp up in the face of loss."

Successful traders embrace losing as part of the process. Being in the game is the life-affirming activity. They don't withdraw because of loss. It hurts if you lose, but it is all about being in the game. The trader who is off target needs not to panic but to focus on what he can do to reduce his risk when the stocks go against him so that he reduces his drawdowns, stays longer with positions that have long-term value, and thereby increases his volatility.

"When I was trading well, a bad day could be viewed as input or warning," said Greg. "It means you need to tweak the strategy. See it as a warning but don't take it as a reflection of yourself."

Part Four

Trading Consistently

Chapter 9

Learning from Your Mistakes

Even master traders aren't perfect. They're human, so they make mistakes. I believe it is possible to improve your trading by learning about the mistakes that you and others encounter, especially since many of the mistakes stem from normal human responses to the uncertain and unpredictable conditions of trading.

For instance, one trader I know had a fabulous seven months and then got smug about it. He lost patience and got involved in a vicious cycle during which he kept picking the wrong tops and bottoms. How could someone have gone from being so in the zone to so *out* of it?

When we talked about his situation, I compared his picks to taking the sucker answer on a multiple choice exam. On such exams there are often five answers, three of which are immediately discarded as wrong. One of the remaining two is the sucker answer. It immediately looks right and is often quickly selected because of the exam taker's anxiety and urgency to select an answer. But it is in fact wrong.

The right answer requires a little more confidence and practice. It requires you to think through the question and choose the answer even though it doesn't beckon you as much as the sucker answer does.

Even the best traders make mistakes. In *Trading to Win*, I devoted some attention to trading mistakes of experienced traders. In this chapter, I examine some additional types of trading mistakes that I have encountered in my work with traders. This examination is to help enlarge your perspective about the potential stumbling blocks you may encounter in the trading arena.

Picking Tops or Bottoms

One mistake traders make is to try to pick tops or bottoms. If a trader thinks a stock, which is moving up, is about to hit its top and turn around, he may short it in order to get as much profit as he can as the price of the stock drops from its high. Picking bottoms is just the opposite. A stock may be moving downward, and a trader, thinking that the stock is about to turn, will buy it near what he thinks is the bottom of the range.

The problem with both of these moves is that no trader can know in advance where a stock will change direction. If he picks a top and sells short, but the trade continues to move upward, then the trader will lose money. If he picks a bottom and buys a stock that continues to move down, he will also lose money. Both these moves can be very costly.

The psychological motivation to pick tops and bottoms is often very hard to combat. Like that sucker answer mentioned at the beginning of this chapter, traders are drawn to what looks like easy ways to make money, especially when they may be behind and are looking for quick profits. But when a trader picks a top or bottom, it's actually because he can't tolerate the uncertainty and isn't willing to wait to see where the trade is going before she steps in.

A master trader controls these impulses, basing her movements on information and strategy instead of emotional guesses. To get the maximum profit out of a trade, she will wait until a rising stock turns before shorting and wait until a falling stock begins moving up before buying. Of course, since a trader must short a stock on an uptick, she has to wait until the stock turns downward and then upward one tick in order to be able to short, all of which means she has to calculate it is going down, decide to short, and then wait for an uptick.

Even if the master trader misses the first move of the trade, at least she trades on the actual movement of the stock and is more patient than the trader who is picking tops and bottoms. Again, to trade in the zone you must follow the strategy you created before entering a trade and not allow your emotions to determine your moves.

Case Studies

A combination of factors (such as anxiety, infatuation with certain stocks, thoughts of hitting a home run, and fantasies of easy money) led Art to short stocks before they had run their full course. He experienced much pain because stocks he shorted continued to go up, forcing him to cover. Art simply couldn't ride out his anxiety and wait for the stocks to stop moving up before he decided to short. Art needed to overcome his anxiousness so that he could make the trade even when it didn't look quite right. Trading correctly requires a willingness to be uncomfortable, and Art was intolerant of discomfort. He just wanted to get it over with.

"I was at $9 million before it went down. Now I am at $7 million. I started to think about the money, and I got less disciplined," said Art. "I was willing to do stupid things to get back to the $9 million. I didn't have the discipline to ignore the market and not do anything. I thought, 'I have to make some money, and this is the quick way to do it.' This process of picking the tops has given me a lot of pain."

To trade in the zone, the process takes longer. A master trader has a reason to short a stock. He doesn't pick tops to get rid of anxiety. He waits until the upward movement seems to have slowed down or stopped. A great trader doesn't short a stock just because it's going up or buy it because it's going down. The master trader buys more if his positions are working and gets out when positions aren't working.

"Usually I am wrong and that creates more discomfort," admitted Art. "When I am right and add to my position or initiate a new position, it's already too late. I have dug myself into a hole. I only make a little back. The master trader waits until he is right and then pounces on it. My discomfort is to see a stock go from 50 to 80. Instead of selling it short, I need to stay with it and watch it go to 90. I can't dispute what the market is doing with the stock. I can't get impatient."

Some traders pride themselves on being contrarians by going against the tide, but the true contrarian buys stocks when there are indicators that the stocks aren't going up any more, not just because of his emotional discomfort or impulsiveness.

Randy, for example, considers himself a contrarian who prefers to short stocks when they are down and buys stocks when they look like they can't go up anymore. In fact, his basic approach is to try to pick tops and scale into shorts before they have run their full distance. On the long side, he tries to scale in at the bottom and often gets in before a stock has fully dropped.

A closer look at Randy's tactics suggests that he is impulsive and being lured in by the bet. He often shorts stocks with minimal information, without looking for major structural weaknesses. In effect, he is not finding good rationales for pricing his shorts.

"Sell your losers early and ride your winners," reiterated one trader. "Do not try to pick tops and bottoms. This market rewards you if you go with the flow. It punishes you more for bad habits. If you pick a top and you are wrong or you try to short at the top, you will get killed."

To deal with this trading mistake, you can learn to ride out your discomfort by using it as a signal to be more aware. Instead of trading to get rid of the discomfort, you should hold on and bide your time. You need to resist the temptation of the quick fix. To trade in the zone, you have to be more cautious and wait for more certainty. Success requires discipline and the ability to tolerate anxiety and uncertainty.

Holding on to Losers

A common problem among inexperienced and experienced traders alike is a tendency to hold on to positions too long. When traders won't let go, they are not only risking the chance of losing capital, they are also tying up capital and therefore missing potential money-making opportunities elsewhere.

"I initiate well but don't liquidate well," said one fixed income trader. "I don't liquidate when it is about to reverse. I understand intellectually what to do. I have trading signals that should take away judgment and emotions. I should get out when the trade first reverses, but I don't."

"The catalyst would come and go, and I would still be there," said another trader. "I need to move when the catalyst moves. I am staying with names too long. I am not as quick to pull the trigger if it moves against me."

According to Terry, the most natural defense is to hold on to positions, generally out of a fear of missing the move. His view is that he makes most of his money in clumps and therefore is inclined to hold on to big positions even when the value of the stock is dropping. More subtly, he starts getting invested in the excitement of reaching his target and loses sight of the fact that his strategy is no longer consistent with his target and that he has to pare down. Usually by the time he is paring down, it is already too late, and he is angry about what he allowed to happen.

Traders who hold on to losers need to focus more on their *daily* targets rather than trying to save money or get it back by holding on indefinitely until something returns to where it ought to be. Such wishful thinking keeps them from being fully in the game.

Case Study

In basketball, Moe is an aggressive player. He keeps pressing and trying harder and is often rewarded with the best shot. In trading, his perseverance causes problems. Moe holds his positions too long, even after they have reached their target numbers, hoping to make more. But then, instead of being nimble and getting out when the stock reverses, he sits there. He watches, paralyzed in amazement, as the stock goes down. He needs to go back to basics and decide on an exit point for taking his profit. This decision means controlling the emotion of greed that often sets in and leads him to want to make more profit than is there. He has to take his profit and not get caught up in the ego-driven impulse to hit home runs. Such nimbleness takes experience and a willingness to face the reality of the trade and not use it to enhance his own self-image.

There are actually a variety of reasons traders hold on to losers. In the following, I review just a few of them in an effort to expand on their psychological origins.

Being too Loyal

Sometimes a trader simply loves the company too much. He is too attached or too loyal. "My strength is my weakness," said Samuel. "I love the company. I feel guilty selling stocks I know so well."

To trade in the zone, traders cannot allow a sense of loyalty to hold them back. They have to read the supply and demand dimensions of the tape and catch the wave of buying and selling.

"Ultimately, all we do is trade supply and demand shifts, the story, the change of story, and so forth," said one trader. "Our ability to profit comes from being on the right side of those shifts, not from loving anything."

"I get too attached to it and trade it two or three times until I finally get it right," said Nina, a bright young assistant who had started to trade her own account in the last six months. "Sometimes enough is enough and I have to take the stock off the screen literally so I am not distracted by the stock blinking on moves. Otherwise, it keeps catching my eye, and I keep thinking I've got to get back in."

Remember, your feelings about the company don't mean anything fundamentally. If the buyers are buying it, even if the earnings are lousy, it is likely to be in an upward momentum. However, if the earnings are good, they may be selling it off, and the price may be dropping. It doesn't matter. The key to success is to see what the market is telling you about the stock and then go after it. Give more credence to what is happening than to your attachment to the company.

Saving Face

Other traders hold on to losers out of a sense of egotism. They want to prove their original decision was right, and curiously, the more they lose, the more convinced they become about the validity of their premises.

For example, Kyle was losing quite a bit in one stock because of what he believed was a negative rumor about the company. He was convinced that, with the current business model, the company would succeed in the long run. Unfortunately, he was wrong.

"I love to be right," he said. "That's why I hold on too long to trades in which I should get flat."

Some traders hold on to losers in an effort to get it just right—making themselves appear more competent. Brent constantly waits for the precise price before acting. He didn't want to short a stock at 43 but waited for 45, the perfect level. The stock dropped to 30, and he missed his trade. He concentrates so much on reducing his losses or his potential for losses that he misses a big chance for profitability.

As he noted, "My analysis and control are killing me. I am squandering opportunities."

There should always be a reason for your trading moves. A decision should never be made in an effort to protect your ego.

Case Study
Terry stays in losing trades because he doesn't want to admit he is wrong and doesn't want to give up another "arrow in his quiver." He should have covered a large European stock when he knew it was going up. He thought there would be sellers in the United States, but when they didn't appear he should have covered.

"I knew it was up for a bad reason, and I thought it would go down," he said. "Then it didn't go down. At some point I knew it was going down, but I still thought it was a decent short for tomorrow."

By covering it, Terry would have admitted it wasn't going to work. By holding the position overnight, he was not accomplishing anything but postponing being wrong. In actual fact, covering would have reduced his losses. If the stock took an upward turn, he could almost always have gotten in again the next day.

When Terry considered this pattern of not getting out of losers, he realized that losses like these added up to a substantial amount of lost profit over the course of the year. He needed to bring more consciousness to his trading and not be governed so much by his automatic or habitual inclination of not covering his shorts and holding them for the next day in order to save face.

Keeping the Stub Ends

Another form of holding occurs when traders retain a portion of a stock after they have sold off the majority of a larger position. They hold on to the so-called stub end of the trade for no other reason than to have at least a little piece of the stock in the event that it turns into a bigger opportunity. This habit ties up a large amount of capital that can be used more profitably elsewhere and may also be the source of additional losses if the stub end continues to move downward.

"Stub ends kill you," said Earl. "They reduce the overall profitability of the trade. It is a matter of latent greed or laziness."

Case Study

Lowell always holds on to a little bit of a stock (even after a capitulation sell-off) instead of following his strategy of getting out and buying the stock after the capitulation. Ideally, he intends to "short, cover, and then go long," but instead holds on to some because of a need to "be right" and to "be prepared for all eventualities."

"I don't know if it's conviction or to be right or to just leave something on the sheets. I am covering my ass, hiding stupid things on the sheets for no reason. I want to be right if even for a little bit. It happens on both sides in my longs and shorts," he said. "It's the same in my personal life. I can't throw things out. I have a little room at home for the junk I collect. I need to learn to completely get out of positions once I decide to get out. Hopefully, keeping the goal in mind will give me the impetus to change this habit so I can get completely out of my positions as they are dropping and then get back in when they turn around. This will save me quite a bit of expense and bring me closer to my targets."

Averaging Down

Some traders not only hold on to a losing trade but buy more of a stock as it is dropping, rationalizing that by paying less for the stock they are lowering the average price of the stock. Of course, this is fine if the stock moves up, but if it doesn't and they stay in the losing position, they will lose more money and not get the benefit of averaging down. A trader should decide on a stopping point for risk management purposes, and when that point is reached she should get out of losing positions—without rationalizing her mistakes by averaging down.

Averaging down is a psychologically risky move at best. Even when a trader does it for the right reasons, he must beware of the inclination to experience the decline in price as a "loss" even though it was consciously chosen. Doing so may compel him to sell too soon when the stock reverses direction and moves back to its original price. Relieved that he has eliminated the "loss," he may not hold on as the stock advances in price. Therefore he may not get the full benefit of the upswing move.

If a trader has "done his homework" and is justified by the knowledge that the fundamentals are sound, that there is a good story that has not changed, that the dropping price does not indicate a significant change in the stock's value, or that there is a good reason for the stock to drop temporarily, then averaging down could make sense.

"I get emotional. Even though I intentionally buy more as certain stocks drop in price because I know the fundamentals are good, I still experience the drawdown as a loss and then try to get out of a stock as it moves up," said Randy. "I rationalize it as it goes down, but I still feel pressure to get out of it as it moves up. It's a mistake. Averaging down to save yourself is different than averaging down because you are investing in it. Take the loss when it is not a good situation but when you are building up a position. When it goes up, remember it is going where you want it to go. Ride the profitability. If a trader is averaging down for the right reason, the key to making it a successful trade still lies within his psychological ability to ride out a big drawdown and then let the profit run to the max."

Regardless of the reason, to overcome a tendency to hold losers, a trader must go back to following a goal-directed strategy. The value of a goal is that it gives you a reason for getting out of the trade. If you are not motivated by the number, you stay in a trade hoping for "the big one." But if it goes in another direction, eventually you lose your money and then you may spend the next trade trying to recoup.

One way to stay on target and overcome the tendency to hold losers is through organization. Earl, an experienced portfolio manager did just this by developing a spreadsheet of his positions and key variables relating to his positions so that he could determine in advance when to add to his positions and when to sell them off. His spreadsheet included variables such as:

- Cost versus current price.
- Target return in dollars.
- Risk in dollars.
- How many days to be in the trade.
- Percent of capital to use for specific trades.
- Upside and downside.
- Current profit and loss on the position.

"Refer to the sheet during the day," said Earl. "If it is up two and it is not on the sheet, we should have it on the sheet. All the decisions should be understood and kept on the sheet."

The key point is that prices don't lie. Don't guess. Watch the movement of the stock and trade according to a strategy, not emotion.

Failing to Take Profits

Failure to ride out a large portion of a stock's move is another common problem that occurs when traders sell too soon—before a trade has run its course and the maximum amount of profit has been reached. Traders who make this mistake are often so anxious to make a profit that they exit the position too soon.

The anxious or inexperienced trader may be too impatient to act and may not wait for the stock to tell him where it is going. He may be drawn into responding to random day-to-day movements rather than to real catalysts or incremental bits of information. He needs to notice his fear or reactivity and base his trading on what he knows about the stock and its trading pattern rather than on his emotions.

Case Studies

Because Peter was not able to tolerate the wide swings in stocks, he was getting anxious and being forced out of trades too early. He was, therefore, missing a big part of the swing.

"I get scared of the stock market," said Peter. "I don't want to lose money. That's what gets me out of the trade. My rational mind knows it is stupid. It is a good trade, but I don't like feeling uncomfortable. That's a problem I have to get over. I have great ideas. I have to get over the hump of worrying about the market. It takes me out of everything. I got this stock. I sold it yesterday because I thought the market was collapsing. I made four points in it. It's up another ten."

Currently, Peter is trading in terms of his interpretation of the market through the lens of his anxiety. He decides to get in a trade because of some X factor. Then, when he gets frightened, Peter sees that X factor totally differently. He lets his emotions color his interpretation. He needs to see his reaction as a separate event. He must view the stock independently of the way he is feeling.

"If I am up in something, I want to take the profit," he said "because if I don't sell, and then it collapses, that is frustrating. I want to avoid that happening at all costs."

Peter needs to learn how to separate the stock movement from his anxiety and his interpretation (that the market is collapsing) from his decision to take the trade. He needs to learn to make decisions in terms of a larger principle—the target or goal to which he has committed himself.

In order to do this, Peter needs to reframe the experience. Let's suppose there is an event. The stock is moving. Peter starts to react. His heart starts beating faster. He begins to develop an interpretation. The market is collapsing. Peter should stop right there. That interpretation—that the market is collapsing—is an interpretation of his feelings, not the event itself.

Like Peter, you may become anxious. You, too, may start to think catastrophic thoughts and make a decision in the moment of reactivity to get out. You must recognize each of these variables as separate and tune them down as if they were controlled by separate dials. Slow your pulse. Think calmly. This lesson came hard for Peter.

Peter had to discover what he had "invested" in being scared. What did he get for being scared? Sympathy. Attention. A rationalization for not being responsible. Peter had to understand that there was no validity to his interpretations. Over time, he learned that he could compensate for his reactivity by knowing more about the stocks. He turned his reaction into a counterintuitive signal so that he could recognize when to get bigger instead of getting out too soon.

Another trader, Ivan, had a similar problem. Ivan's stock selection was excellent. His percentage of winning trades was 54.8 percent. But, he too needed to learn to hold longer and to get into bigger positions when he had conviction.

One of the reasons that he was not as profitable as he could be was that he was getting out of positions very rapidly and taking a half dollar of profit from trades where he lacked conviction. Although his trade size was getting bigger, he was unable to let profits run and had a very small spread between his average winning trade and his average losing trade. His average winning per share is .23 and average loss per losing trade is .20.

An aspect of this is that 40 percent of his trades were with the DOT (designated order turnaround, a computerized order execution system), which only accounted for 23 percent of his profit and loss (P&L). He saved his "idea" trades for the brokers, which accounted for 53 percent of his profitability but a much smaller volume of his trades.

"I am always too quick to take my profits when I have size," he said. "When I have 25,000, I can ride it out. When it is up 2, it can go up another 2 tomorrow. But with size, when it is up one quarter, that's 50 grand. I start to think of the profit. When I am in a big position, I get spooked out and try to get back what I lost in other positions by scalping a quick profit. This is a maturity thing. I need to learn to delay gratification."

If you are like Peter or Ivan and are taking profits too fast, you too can learn to stay in trades longer. At the moment you are getting uncomfortable, you have to separate what you are feeling from what the market is doing. Remember your original ideas. Talk yourself through the anxiety. See what is really happening. Distinguish how you are feeling from what the market is doing.

Make your decisions on the basis of your original plan, not your anxiety. In the heat of the moment, things seem to happen instantaneously but, in fact, when you make these distinctions you can begin to react more intelligently.

If you tend to get out too soon, try getting more fundamental information so as to gain conviction to hold longer and to be able to sit still and wait until the stock comes to fruition while trading around your core position. An additional suggestion is to focus this effort on selected stocks or a limited number of sectors so that you can build expertise and a storehouse of knowledge about the stocks you are trading.

Bidding for Stocks

Sometimes traders lose out on good trades because they put in limit orders to buy stocks at specified prices rather than market orders to buy them at whatever price is available. Although there is nothing wrong with trying to get a good deal, you must weigh the cost of the stock versus the amount of profit that you think can be made and consider the urgency in which the stock is needed. If there's news, there's usually a greater need to pay up to get the stock, whereas if there's no news, you may be able to wait.

Bidding for stocks becomes a mistake when you lose opportunities for a big profit. This situation especially occurs in fast-moving stocks. In those cases, it may be wiser to take the offer and pay up for a stock, especially if has already started moving up.

Case Study
Edgar described an incident where he didn't move quickly enough. "The market was 119½, 119¾. It kept bouncing around," Edgar explained. "I bid 119¼ for 15,000 shares of a large-cap industrial company. It traded 119⅜ and then traded up to 125. If I had paid up I would have gotten it. Instead I missed it. I was trying to save one quarter of a point. The big players will tell you that if you want to

be in it, then get in it. If you don't want to be in it, then don't be in it. That's a discipline. A lot of my losses were because I didn't move quickly enough."

Randomness can be minimized with an information edge. When placing a bid, traders need to be looking for incremental bits of information: events, timing, benchmarks, announcements. Stocks have their largest moves at pressure points, which are influenced by catalytic events that are deviations from the norm—some event that leads to a difference between consensus and reality. That adjustment causes a shift in the information that is factored into the stock and changes the stock price. A master trader knows the facts and the relevance of the facts and does not lose out on a big profit because he's squabbling to save a few cents.

Relying on Intuition

Although the best traders rely on a combination of intuition and information, it is a mistake to become overly attached to your own notions. When you have a notion to react to what is happening, make sure you get all the information you can and don't get wedded to your ideas.

"You are not in the business of pontificating," said Reggie, an experienced portfolio manager. "You have to figure out whether you are stating hard facts or notions. Notions are different from drilling down on why things are really cheap and identifying catalysts. Has anyone checked your thinking? What if your thinking is wrong? You are better off dealing with the facts. You are in the business of taking low-risk shots with a high-return potential and can't buy into your own theories."

"When you create a portfolio, see what your Achilles heel is," he continued. "You may want to know your tendency and then get another trader to check you. Look back over 10 years statistically to see how your trades have done. Forget what you think. See what happened. How would you change your portfolio?"

"Traders have to be careful about making suppositions. You can't buy into random correlations or statistical quirks. You need to check your facts so that when you make a supposition it is based on more than intuition."

Some traders think it is cool to be right. They like to consider themselves the smartest. The master traders know they are not always going to be right. They recognize their own failings and build around them.

"I used to do trades like that," said Reggie. "Your ego is tied up in making these calls. When you are right, it is a rush. When you are wrong, you get down on yourself. It is unbearable. The reality is you are not that great when you are right and not that bad when you are wrong. You are just a human being trying to do the best you can do. The key is knowing what you can do and doing what works. It happens. My ego isn't tied up in that stuff anymore."

Overtrading

When traders are carrying more stocks than they can reasonably manage, a new problem is created—overtrading. When a trader is unable to stay focused because he has too many irons in the fire, a variety of other mistakes can also begin to take place. He will then not only lose money by mishandling the trades he has, but he will also lose money in missed opportunities.

For example, Edgar is losing a lot of small amounts that add up. He holds things overnight without good reason, and then when they gap down in the morning he is off to a bad start. He doesn't have catalysts and is trading very volatile stocks when he should be trading his retail groups, which he understands better.

Edgar can't get into the zone because he has lost sight of his target. He is involved with too many companies that he has not been studying. Because he has stretched his resources to the limit, he is unable to obtain all the information he needs to make intelligent trading decisions. He is concentrating on how much money he has lost or what profit he could have made instead of how to get back on track.

There is no set number of trades that a master trader has. Each trader is different, and some traders can handle more trades than others. The number of trades you carry depends on your capital, your experience, and your ability to focus. Portfolio managers, of course, carry more trades than the normal trader. A day trader most likely carries fewer trades than a professional.

Sometimes it helps to have another trader or manager review your trades with you in order to determine whether you are handling too many. The critical issue is to know when enough is enough and to get rid of trades that are unprofitable so as to maximize your wins in other areas.

Case Studies

James's overtrading is causing him to lose focus and has contributed to his inability to pull the trigger at the right time. He keeps getting out of good trades just to reduce the number of his positions. Yet, he is conflicted about getting out of losing positions. He thinks he can't stand the pain.

"I had 14 positions, but I was taking money off the table," he said. "There was nothing wrong with the stocks. They closed a lot higher. I sold them because I wanted to lighten up. I have to sell something because I am not comfortable holding it. I sell out if I am wrong or right. I have too many positions."

For James, the solution is to take smaller bites and let them fully develop. When he reduces his positions, he can pay closer attention to them and make as much profit as is available from the trade.

Justin is another trader whose statistics also suggested that he could increase his profitability by reducing the number of securities that he held at any one time, increasing the value of positions he held overnight, and expanding his holding periods. These steps would correct for his tendency to overtrade and to perform poorly in volatile markets.

A solution that helped Justin was to focus on a single sector—consumer goods. By doing so he began to get more ideas, learned how to rely on catalysts, and recognized the value of staying focused on his own trades and not being distracted by what else was going on in the room.

Reviewing Mistakes

Obviously, each trading situation is unique, and it is impossible to present a defined set of "rules" that cover each decision that has to be made. Every trade has a different set of fundamental and technical analyses, different catalysts, and different time factors. And in reality, most traders make a combination of errors, not just one.

For that reason, I want to outline one more case scenario before ending this chapter. In this situation, I closely examine the variety of mistakes one trading team made and how they changed their strategy in order to improve their trading game.

Case Study
Over the course of four months, Mario and Lucas worked to develop a profitable investment style and partnership based on blending long-term valuation trades with short-term, catalyst-driven, high-velocity trades. In so doing, they identified numerous problems that they sought to overcome.

First, they found that they were being governed by the short-term inclination of trying to kill it instead of following a more manageable and risk-controlled template.

"When we reviewed our trading in July and August of 1999, we found that 80 percent of our mistakes were attributable to being too big, too fast, and not scaling in," said Lucas.

The team took value or medium-term catalyst positions and immediately grew them to significant size in the portfolio. This strategy often led to a large decline in the price of the shares with no room to scale or average down. As there were no short-term catalysts, getting big so fast was disastrous for the P&L, leading them to hunker down or start to sell.

A second major problem was failure to scale out as a stock was reaching its target, which led to some situations in which they failed to take their profits and then watched as the stock moved down again. Here certain trades, which were put on in anticipation of a catalyst they predicted would trigger buying of a stock, actually materialized, but instead of taking their profit, they held on, turning these trade opportunities into core positions. To compound the error, instead of buying more as the stock dipped, they held on or even bought more as it moved back up, trying to capture some of the momentum move in the stock.

They would purchase or short a stock with a particular catalyst in mind (most often short term), average in as the position went against them, and then, when the original catalyst failed to materialize, continue to hold the position. They justified this action by calling the position "value" or "medium-term." The result was usually a busted trade that they bottom (or top) ticked getting out. Additionally, they would pick tops and bottoms with no catalyst in sight.

Another problem they identified was their inclination to change their theses in the middle of a trade.

"We would put something on the sheet for a reason, but then the event occurred, and it wasn't the catalyst we thought it would be. So all of a sudden we would think of another reason why owning or being short this stock would work. We had changed our thesis."

For example, XYZ was a bad trade for this team. They were up $750,000, but they ended down $70,000. They didn't rigorously check their thought process, not taking liquidity when they could, not having bought it when it first went down, not getting out when the thesis didn't work, and then finally capitulating when the stock was below where they bought it originally. They held on and still owned 250,000 shares with the view that newsprints were getting better. It was a case study of failure. They didn't follow their game plan.

Like moths to flame, they put shorts on the sheet when stocks had a big run or started buying when the stocks had collapsed. Nine of ten times, however, they didn't have a reason for the run to stop or the collapse to end; and the shorts in question were usually good companies, the longs bad. This was a particularly dangerous game for their blend of investment style. Finally, Randy and Lucas would get out too soon, failing to take their profit.

"We would develop an idea to go long or short a particular group or stock based on some near to medium-term catalyst. We averaged into the position well and stuck through the losses associated with this particular form of trading. Then, as soon as the shares started to move in our direction, we quickly took the profits and watched as the thesis continued to unfold as we thought it would. The result was that we were often breaking even on these trades, or, at best, taking small gains for a disproportionate amount of risk."

Cognizant of these mistakes, this team worked to correct the above foregoing themes and transform their investment style into something bigger and better. Unfortunately, it is easy in the heat of battle to forget the plan and act impulsively.

"We got off target because we were looking at these grandiose $1 million dollar bets," said Mario. "The next thing you know we are down $1 million during the day, and then we get skewered. We were not waiting for the bet to go right before piling in. If we go for the daily target, it changes our discipline and our timing. We were also getting too intellectually arrogant. We were reluctant to talk to sell-side analysts from big firms. We thought we didn't need to speak to them. We thought we were too good for them. We didn't want to invest in their ideas because if they worked, it was their idea."

Going further, Lucas added, "There is a rational basis for the price and the multiples, and we should keep assessing it so that we can make intelligent decisions and maximize our profitability. A strategy is critical because it helps keep us from falling prey to the emotional impact of fear at the bottom and greed at the top."

The optimal strategy is to take your profit as you get near to your target so that by the time you reach your target you are out of the trade. You do not need to hold on and experience the fluctuations associated with short-term volatility. This way you can capture short-term profits and maximize your overall rate of return on your capital.

Lucas described the progress they made after reviewing their mistakes and trying to correct their strategy:

"We are trying to measure the conviction versus the catalyst versus the size of position. We are trying to do this with a position spreadsheet. We are avoiding illiquid names. We even go so far as to play index trades or investment for liquidity purposes if the ideas we have are thematic rather than stock-specific."

"We now try to have a reason for everything on the sheet. If we are in something for a specific reason, we get completely out when that reason disappears or changes. We go over the positions two or three times a day and remind ourselves why we're there and what our target prices are."

"We also focus on the 'fat pitches.' We've found that the temptation to short the high-flyers can be mitigated by just staying away and waiting for downside catalysts. We also move to short lower beta stocks where we can get an edge."

"We try to keep playing the thesis as long as it's intact. We need to press our bets, and this is the best way to do it. We can continue to trade around the thesis, but if the directional bet is, for example, long the OSX [Oil Service Stock Index], we'll look to trade into the group over time on the long side until the thesis disappears."

This team's experiences and observations demonstrate the significance of the daily goal for the astute trader who uses it as a lens for determining what he must do. The goal helps you to focus on the important issues so that you don't get caught up in your own intellectual arrogance. It forces you to come face-to-face with the natural resistance to change in order to maximize performance. Moreover, the more you stretch to achieve your goals, the more capable you become of bringing more of yourself into play.

The master trader is continually focusing on a larger target, which leads him to continually adapt to new procedures and methods designed to reach the target. To keep going in the face of great success or loss, he has to keep defining his targets and his strategy. By doing so he keeps pulling more out of himself.

In every situation, the psychological processes that a trader must consider are the same. To avoid making costly mistakes, a trader must always consider the facts—the information that he has gathered, the news events that are taking place. In every situation, he must take note of his own emotions and control how his feelings influence his actions.

And in every situation the trader needs to trade for a daily goal and follow a predetermined strategy.

Although it is not always possible to call the *exact* high or low, this last piece of advice is crucial to avoiding many of the mistakes discussed in this chapter. By choosing to wait on the market for indicators on when to buy and sell and by complying with the stop losses you have set before entering the trade, you can minimize your losses and maximize your winners. Mistakes are inevitable, but learning from your mistakes in an effort to prevent repeating them is a crucial part of trading in the zone.

Chapter 10

Overcoming Psychological Obstacles

Meet Risky Robert and Cautious Ken. They are prime examples of two distinct personalities. Let me tell you a little about them and see if you identify with either one.

Risky Robert obviously loves risk, novelty, and variety. He seeks intense experiences such as mountain climbing and downhill skiing. The more ambiguous the situation—a new route up a dangerous mountain, a new double-back diamond ski run he's never been on—the happier he is. Because Robert thinks he can control his fate, he is "inner directed." He is spurred on not by others but by his own personality. He believes he can handle anything life might throw at him, and he loves the challenge of it all. Robert is, in short, what psychologists call a Type T personality—a thrill seeker.

On the other hand, we have Cautious Ken. He is just the opposite. In winter, you might find Ken on the cross-country ski trails, but most likely he'll stick to the treadmill at the gym, and he'll be there faithfully at the same time of day, the same day of the week, every week. Ken likes predictability and stability. He does not like risk but prefers the certainty of regularly scheduled developments in a familiar setting. He likes to have everything under control. Ken is a Small T personality—a risk-averse person.

So, are you more like Risky Robert or Cautious Ken? There's no right answer. Actually, you probably have elements of both these personality types and can learn much about your trading by identifying these and other common behavioral patterns and by understanding how those patterns influence your propensity for or against risk.

The best traders have usually developed traits from both personality types. Like good adventurers they like the mastery that comes from conquering difficult situations but understand the importance of being prepared beforehand. They want to find the place between high and low risk where there is challenge enough to stimulate but not so much that it is overwhelming. They also have learned to monitor other emotional responses and habits so they can be as unencumbered as possible and can bring all of their intellect, courage, discipline, and desire to bear in order to trade in the zone.

No one is born with the perfect personality for trading, and every personality brings with it both good traits and bad traits. In fact, the very thing that is a trader's strength can sometimes be a weakness.

For example, Ric is an analyst turned trader who is too controlled and overly cautious. He doesn't trust the markets and is, therefore, hesitant to start trading with a decent position.

It is "tough to know every detail or to trade on a few details," he said.

Of course, being cautious is reasonable. It is not necessarily a bad thing. When a trader is cautious, he, like Ric, pays attention to details. But while attention to detail is essential for first-class analysis, excessive analysis can inhibit the ability to pull the trigger. And if a trader is unable to pull the trigger, he cannot trade in the zone.

Passivity is another kind of personality problem. Mason, for example, was trying to mask his leadership. He was reluctant to demand performance from the analysts working for him. Mason was too concerned about being a good guy and was not looking at what needed to be done in order to produce results consistent with his objectives. In effect, he was passively going along with other analysts' idiosyncratic work and wasn't being as directive as he could be.

Traders need to identify psychological obstacles that may result from their long-standing personality traits in order to structure their trading strategy independently of them or at least in such a way as to minimize the less desirable and less flexible components. Although it is often psychologically uncomfortable to rein in these types of impulses, unless a trader does so, the obstacles will not disappear, and the trading pattern will persist.

In this chapter, I outline some of the major psychological obstacles that appear among traders by way of illuminating some of the behavioral patterns that may influence your trading and which may be keeping you from trading in the zone.

Letting Go of Seller's Remorse

Seller's Remorse is not an uncommon psychological response. It is experienced by most traders, at one time or another, as a result of trying to rethink a past decision. Traders who fall prey to this problem spend a considerable amount of time and energy obsessing about a position they have sold. They worry that the position might still go up and that they, therefore, could have sold it at a better price if only they had held on to it. In effect, remorse eats away at the confidence of the trader. He starts focusing on what he has done, thinking about his mistakes and how much money he could have made. This initiates a self-cycling pattern of negative thinking that preoccupies him and disables him from trading in the zone.

A trader may experience Seller's Remorse when he actually did make a mistake by trying to pick a top, shorting or selling a stock as it is going up thinking it is about to turn, only to see it continue to move up. Here too, even though it is useful to review trades, obsessive self-criticism rather than assessment and tweaking one's strategy rarely proves productive.

When a trader experiences Seller's Remorse and watches a stock continue to go up, he may impulsively decide to chase after it as it moves up and buy more of it at a higher price. Although there are times that it is wise to buy a stock at a higher price, if you enter a trade in an effort to eliminate your regret at having sold earlier, you are trading for the wrong reason. In addition, to avoid the uncomfortable feelings of Seller's Remorse, some traders compound their problems by holding on to losing trades.

Case Study

When I first began working with Kurt, a highly successful trader, he regularly experienced Seller's Remorse and frequently lost confidence when facing a losing trade, which caused him to lose even bigger. Specifically to avoid the distress of selling something and then having it go back up, he stayed with bad trades hoping against hope that his positions would improve and rationalizing to himself that he was lining himself up for profitability. In reality, he was simply trading to avoid the negative emotions of Seller's Remorse.

"In deconstructing down days, I hold on when it is not working," he said. "I make plenty of money, but I lose too much as well. I have $20 million worth of good trades and $10 million worth of bad trades. I make too many marginal trades and try to turn what I call 'good' trades into 'very good' trades when it oftentimes can't be done."

Fortunately Kurt had some positive experiences in golf where he played tough and wasn't bothered by bad shots. Rather he had learned to keep focusing on the next play. In trading he said, "Bad trades go on, and you have to manage them first to avoid losses." So, Kurt began to think consciously about his mental approach to golf to help him focus more on his trading opportunities than on his failures.

By keeping track of his trades, he soon realized that he could get out of losing trades and then get back in if they again turned upward. The exception was for situations where he knew the fundamentals and could discount the temporary impact of some macro or news events that influenced the market action in the stock.

After a number of months, Kurt could state confidently: "I have learned not to press my trades as much. I am waiting for good trades to come to me. I had to learn that I could sell stocks and know that I could get back into them. In mornings, I have to go back to good trades, add more recent ones, and put myself in the right mental state."

Today Kurt remains conscientious and manages Seller's Remorse by not spending as much time dwelling on past mistakes. When things are going bad, he has learned to put himself in the mind-set of past successes. In this way, he finds it is easier to stop losses and focus on future events.

The key to overcoming Seller's Remorse is to recognize that a "woulda, shoulda, coulda" mind-set is distracting and enervating. Again, as emphasized throughout this book, to trade in the zone you need to focus on a defined goal and then develop a strategy consistent with it in terms of specific entry and exit points. You also must be mindful of taking your profits and be patient enough to ride out the movement of a stock. If you know the range in which it trades and have done the fundamental work, you will know when to sell or when to short a stock or, if wrong, will have a controlled exit point.

Trading in the zone means not getting caught up in the speculation of what might have been. Notice your thinking and start refocusing on your daily objective and what you need to do to maximize your results. When you are in the zone, you don't allow your mistake to drag you down. You remain in a positive, proactive state of mind even when you are not doing well.

As I mentioned in Chapter 9, every trader makes mistakes, but to trade in the zone, you must recognize your mistakes and learn from them without letting them destroy your trading style. You must use these mistakes to increase your level of control, without trying to recoup your loss in one fell swoop. It is also critical to spend time meditating on past successful trades before you start the day so that you can get into the right frame of mind for maximizing your skills. You need to trade similarly to your successful days, thereby reducing your distractions and emotions. By recreating a positive mental mind-set, you can maximize your skills and trade in a framework of success, not out of a sense of guilt or regret.

Perfectionism and Paralysis

Information overload sometimes leads to decision paralysis in traders who get caught up in their own labyrinthine thoughts. The ability to assess a balance sheet, which can be a strength, may at times become a liability if it leads to overanalyzing. The search for 100 percent information and 100 percent certainty about any situation will stymie any trader. You will never have 100 percent of the information available, and looking for it will make you buy after all the good news is out or sell too late. Traders have to remember that there will always be at least one reason not to trade. A master trader knows how to balance the scales and make his decision based on the weight of the issues.

The self-centered nature of perfectionism manifests itself as an inclination to obsess about potential problems as well as the attitudes, responses, and anticipated criticism of others. Underlying the pattern is a basic motivation not to spend, not to risk, to look good, and not to swing for the fences. There is a basic fear of taking a risk. There is an underlying cautiousness, a reluctance to pay up for things, an emphasis on value, and a concern about being too exposed.

Consider the following questions to determine if perfectionism is a problem for you:

- Are you self-critical?

- Do you view your own efforts as insignificant or insufficient?

- Do you allow the voices from the past or the anticipated criticism of others to get you off your strategy?

- Are you caught up with a range of time-consuming activities that absorb energy and attention and distract you from taking responsibility for the full development of your interests?

- How much energy do you lose in activities set for you by others?

- How easy is it for you to get off your own strategy?

The challenge in working with perfectionist traders is often to get them to do what works. Every trader who battles with this problem requires a unique solution to overcome it.

Some traders simply wait for everything to be "perfect" before they pull the trigger. In effect, they are afraid to enter the realm of uncertainty. They begin to romanticize the past and forget that they were once willing to take risks. For others, perfectionism is characterized by a tendency to get bogged down in too many details and too much analysis. They are afraid to take action in the face of ambiguity and uncertainty, as was the case with Edwin.

Case Studies

Edwin had a tendency to be overanalytical. He understood the nature of the marketplace and the reason why there were so many companies that were good shorts. He did the analysis and found a number of busted companies. Unfortunately, he was paralyzed by his analysis and couldn't implement his ideas successfully. He was afraid that the stock would move up and "squeeze" him after he shorted it, especially if it was a short that had already come down some distance.

He was also confused about long-term and short-term objectives and got very uncomfortable with some of his longer-term shorts because he was worried about near-term or daily profits. Basically Edwin needed to learn to whistle and stand on one leg at the same time, that is, to get daily profitability and extend it when he had the opportunity to make more money.

"I am overanalytical," he admitted. "I keep thinking about issues on every trade which prevent me from acting. I am not following my methodology. I have not harnessed my analysis to my trading. For example, one large-cap food company is in merger talks. Instead of making the calls, I stare at it. I am not acting. I am paralyzed. I should be checking on the news. I should have a calendar of events so that I am prepared for them. The task is to pay attention to the warning signs of the companies I have studied and understand. I still lack the confidence which comes from action."

Although Edwin does a lot of work on his short theses, he doesn't seem to have an organized system for implementing his ideas as well as he might. His line of thought goes on and on, and he remains inactive.

As important as information gathering is, trading in the zone requires trading and not perfect analysis. If you are like Edwin and experiencing the problem of perfectionism and paralysis, you may need to whittle down your trades until you are small enough that you feel comfortable trading again. Obviously, being right is important because you don't want to lose money, but you can only learn how to trade by doing it, not by getting it right beforehand.

Charles has a similar problem. He is an online trader who consulted with me after reading *Trading to Win*. He spent two years taking courses and learning how to trade 30-year treasury bonds. Now that he has set up his system, he finds himself unable to trade.

Charles is highly organized, and his expectations are high. He wants to do 20 contracts a day, but he also wants to be absolutely certain about his trades before he executes them. As a consequence, he has become paralyzed in his efforts.

"I have never had a problem with anything until now," said Charles. "In business I wasn't going to give up. I feel like I am responsible for my results. I see that I am responsible for losing last year."

The very things that helped Charles succeed in his previous management consultant business—his organization, orientation to detail, and controlling nature—are the very things that are holding him back in his trading. The very aspects that help him organize and decide what is essential to trade are actually getting in the way of implementing his trades.

"I have stops, but I get out before my stops are hit," he said. "I take it personally that I made a bad decision. If I made a bad trade, I try to examine it right then and there. Then I get into this self-critical, analytic mode of thinking where I can't trade. When the trading day is over, I retrade the day and see what I could have done differently."

Charles has to learn to crawl before he walks and walk before he runs. A significant part of effective trading is knowing that you will be wrong a lot. Learning to be confidant that you will eventually be right and more effective on your winners allows you to trade in the zone.

The goal is to make money, and it doesn't really matter where Charles begins. He knows what to do. His system works, but he is simply too paralyzed by anxiety to put the trade on. He can begin to get past his fear by first reducing his goal to something more reasonable. Being responsible for his trading means doing what he needs to do to handle the current situation. His current expectations are putting too much pressure on him.

Another option to overcoming this hurdle is to have someone else, a family member or an assistant, place the trade for him or come into the office and help him make the trade. The smartest, most analytic types aren't necessarily the best traders and often function better with a trading assistant who executes the trade. Even in his previous business, Charles had to admit that he couldn't do everything. He sometimes had to delegate certain functions to others. By calling in someone else to place a trade, he can help break the ice and begin working toward his goal. By telling someone else, who is not burdened with the same feelings, he can watch his work take root and grow into a successful trade.

Creating a system is one thing; teaching it is another. Actually, trading is still another. The analytically oriented perfectionist and implementers are different personalities. Charles might be good at getting others to do things and can, therefore, produce results in that manner.

The objective for Charles is to begin to trade. The goal is to make money. A reasonable target for him might be to do one high probability trade of ten contracts. The goal may mean putting on one trade a day, even if he has to bring someone in to actually execute the trade. He has to break through this barrier of paralysis, one way or another. This was a bit challenging for him since it meant relinquishing, at least temporarily, his larger goals and setting up more realistic daily goals.

When a trader is battling this psychological obstacle, the longer he procrastinates, the harder it is to pull the trigger. Trading does not amount to executing with perfect information. In fact, trading in the zone actually requires that traders act with less-than-perfect information in an unpredictable and volatile market.

The "Poor Me" Syndrome

The Poor Me syndrome relates to any one of a number of attitudes that traders adopt so that they are not in touch with their creative potential. It is a form of culturally acceptable egotism that keeps people from trading in the zone.

Basically, some traders sink into depression after a bad day or fall into a socially learned role of losing. After a loss, they act like failures. They go around looking sad, bemoaning their fate, calling attention to the fact that they have lost, leading others to ask frequently, "What happened?" This posture lends itself to receiving sympathy, encouragement, and reassurance from other traders.

"I am like the warrior who likes to demonstrate he can take pain," said one trader. "I take the bruises as war medals. That is a draining way to live."

This phenomenon demonstrates an unconscious barrier to moving on. It's as if the trader cannot go forward to the next event without spending time demonstrating how badly he feels about his failure. If he doesn't beat his chest about how he screwed up, others might think he is too cavalier and doesn't care.

A pattern of self-blame and guilt about bad trades or loss of money applies to a lot of traders who focus on losing. If you are too rushed and quick to try to get your next set of profits to compensate for your losses, you also will miss the bigger picture of what you need to do to succeed over time.

Case Studies
Vincent was a trader who had been steadily losing money in his currency trades. He began to dwell on his losses and see them as a reflection of himself. He, therefore, began to feel very bad about himself and became convinced there were no more opportunities to succeed.

Vincent compounded his problem by discussing his trades with brokers and other traders who were also going through difficult times. Instead of helping encourage him, this discussion only promoted his Poor Me attitude. His depressing and negative attitude carried through on his trades, and he soon began to expect losses. Others expected losses from him as well because losses were all he talked about.

His pessimistic attitude evolved into a self-perpetuating cycle of failure. He experienced a loss, which led to his negative attitude. His negative attitude was further incorporated into his trading behavior when he began discussing his losses with other traders who were losing. Then he, and others, began to expect him to lose, and he did.

Interestingly enough, after an examination of Vincent's trades, we discovered that he was actually finding opportunities, but he was reacting to them in the wrong way. By definition, if he had reversed his actions, he would have made money. There were opportunities, but he was seeing them in reverse. I began to coach Vincent to stop talking about how bad things are and to stop beating his chest. This attitude only invited sympathy and a certain pressure (however subtle) to keep focusing on the negative.

Bruce is another example of a Poor Me trader. He recently lost $10 million dollars after being up $5 million. Afterward, all he kept thinking about for weeks was the length of his losing streak. Again, this negative train of thought only led him to develop a new self-concept based on losing.

Many traders who develop this self-critical syndrome rationalize it as realism. They are only "being honest about their performance," they will say. And honesty is important. You shouldn't try to deny your mistakes, but you shouldn't focus on them either. The trick to overcoming the Poor Me syndrome is to notice what went wrong, correct for it, and then move on to the next trade.

Of course, moving on isn't as easy as it sounds. Vincent, Bruce, and many other traders caught in this cycle get some satisfaction from the sympathy they receive. They may not be aware of it, but they actually enjoy the attention they receive when other traders are commiserating with them.

The Poor Me syndrome also absolves the trader of his responsibility for staying focused and getting centered. The trader accepts the concept of himself as a loser and accepts blame for his performance, and this acceptance becomes an excuse for not focusing on what has to be done to get into the zone. He begins to look at his trading career in a new light—as if the power for his success has been handed over to fate and he is helpless to do anything about it.

Traders who have experienced a loss or a succession of losses must gain enough courage to tell others that they don't want to talk about it. Without taking this step, it can take even longer to give up the burden of this syndrome.

In addition, traders who have experienced big losses can benefit from the advice expounded on earlier in this book:

- Go back to taking smaller positions.

- Make quicker bets.

- Don't try to regain your loss.

- Lower your daily targets to more achievable numbers.

- Start with small wins first.

A practical way of trying to get out of this rut and to get back into the zone is to keep notes in a diary about your feelings correlated with your trades and the markets. Track your feelings as another indicator of what is going on within your trades so that you gain some objectivity about your emotional reaction, but don't interpret your feelings as reality. Don't carry your emotions around with you to the extent that you call them up whenever you need to put the blame on something or when you want sympathy from others.

When you lose, move on to the next trade, without the emotional theatrics, and then spend some time, after the trading day, to examine the trade. Determine whether it should have been done differently. If so, establish safeguards so that the mistake is not repeated. As mentioned in Chapter 8, by tracking your emotions you can help identify them as a piece of data about yourself and then start trading quite independently of these self-absorbing considerations so that you can get back in the zone.

Combating Complacency

Complacency is the enemy of all traders. It comes when things are going too well and you are not being challenged. Complacency often appears after a successful run when you begin to take your success for granted, and it causes you to make mistakes. When you stop being alert, stop analyzing data, stop preparing, and trade without paying attention to your discipline, you are out of the zone and headed toward trouble. Complacency leads to losses and further feelings of frustration and sluggishness, which in turn leads to more mistakes.

Case Study
Donald began trading with the feeling that he had a cushion, which in effect set the stage for a number of big losses. He got too relaxed after success and then tried to force trades.

"I can't allow myself to get complacent or too euphoric," he said. "From my greatest success came my greatest failure. I have to make an effort to stay focused in the face of a half year of success. I tend to think, 'I'm good. I can do what I want.' If I am down 800, I can afford to lose it. I get too cavalier because I am doing well. I stop paying attention."

It takes an internal shift to allow yourself to have money and to not fall into this sluggishness.

"When guys start making $25 million a year," said Sandy, "it isn't easy. Not everyone can handle it. People are making it but will give it away. They believe it was their skill and will do some stupid thing. To handle wins, you really have to be intellectually honest with yourself and your process. Some of that involves maturity and experience, to know when it is luck and when it is skill. Sometimes it is luck as part of the process. You have to respect the market, or it will take the money back."

Complacency often precedes boredom and burnout. Therefore, it is useful to notice when you are feeling this way and take steps to make your trading more interesting. This action may mean simply recommitting to your objectives, or it may involve more work such as making more calls or visiting companies. Then again, if complacency becomes a serious hindrance, it may mean taking a vacation or a short break from your trading responsibilities to regroup.

One thing is certain. Traders who suffer from complacency need to find a partner, mentor, coach, or even a spouse who can help keep them grounded. They need an honest person to remind them of their humanity and their need for discipline.

Inability to Adjust

The market is constantly changing. So, traders who want to stay in the zone must keep reexamining their strategy. Adjusting does not usually require traders to change their strategy. Adjusting to market conditions is, instead, another means of getting back into the zone. A trader needs to look at his strategy and how the market changes have affected his current positions. It means digging in and remaining true to his strategy so as not to sacrifice his discipline and edge, even in the midst of turbulent times.

The master trader is mobile and able to switch directions on a dime. He is able to change what he is doing based on new situations.

"The master trader is particularly good at not getting attached to information or his previous opinion about a stock," said Jon. "He can be in a story, long 250,000 shares, and it is not going well, and he'll get out. He forgets the story until things are better. He is not invested in the story."

A master trader is like Wayne Gretzky. He goes where the puck is going. He manages his risk. There is no ego in the trade. He knows what he is in the trade for. He makes his money. If it looks like an event is over or something has changed, he gets out of the trade. He recognizes what has changed. He is macro and micro oriented. He can move in any direction.

Although many traders follow the path of least resistance and stay in a losing trade because it is initially more comfortable to sit still than to take the loss, the master trader doesn't. The master trader has the discipline to get out and take the smaller loss.

To reach the zone, you too must continually make assessments and consider such questions as:

- Is this price a new high?
- Is there a buying weakness at this new high?
- Is the price volatile?
- Have the bulls become exhausted?
- Is the market about to turn?
- Are the bears getting ready to pounce?
- How long has the price moved in this direction?
- How has it reacted to news?
- How has it gotten to this level, and how long has it stayed there?
- What can all these variables tell me about the price?

The master trader is not worried about what he paid or what his losses have been. He treats each day as separate from other days and each trade as separate from others.

"Good traders admit when they are wrong," said Ed. "They are open-minded. This is a kind of objectivity—knowing when you are wrong."

To succeed, you must be able to maximize the trade and not become fearful. Don't be afraid to keep pushing when you are in a good trade. Be willing to reverse course and go short on something you have been trading long when circumstances change and the information suggests a downturn.

The master trader doesn't scalp the way some other traders do or try to take a profit to make up for losses in other trades. But he may scale down if he sees the profitability being reduced or the risks changing. He is also able to expand beyond the target price when he sees a chance for more profit. This objectivity is the essence of his adaptability.

Case Study

Chris has committed to a $15 million target. Upon doing so, he realized that there were trades that he had previously gotten out of too soon. He now sees where he has missed opportunities to make money and is getting back into some of those trades. With his expanded target, he has a powerful incentive to be disciplined about entry and exit points and to explore other ways of making money.

He is also using mental rehearsal to help him prepare for upcoming trades. He reviews in his mind all possible contingencies and plans how he is going to react to opportunities and obstacles. This mental preparation helps him to react to sudden shifts in events. This practice helped Chris to ride through a recent bout of rumors that caused everyone to short a stock. Chris played it long and proved right. In fact he was as big as he could get. He was ahead of the curve and comfortable with his variant position. Last week he got out of one big position but got right back in it at the twice the size, impelled by his vision of $15 million. He is also trying new things like taking some profits on his winning trades so as to protect his gains and not getting out of the whole trade as he might have done in the past. The best traders are able to be this flexible.

Unfortunately, many traders have difficulty with this distinction and often start performing counterproductively when they are spooked out of their styles by changing markets. The more critical thing is to stick with what has worked before, only slightly adapting your strategy. If you are losing, lower your numbers until you get back in the groove, and build a track record of several consecutive successful weeks before trying to get bigger again.

Case Studies

In the months of April and May 2000, the previously bull market turned downward and many momentum traders who had made a lot of money in technology stocks, software stocks, and other high flying stocks began to have problems. They had difficult trading in the bear market. They had little experience in shorting stocks. They were frazzled, and they didn't make the money they had made before. The following traders had trouble adjusting to the change in the tape and the market direction. Let's learn a little about each of their cases.

Stick with your strategy. Trevor was no longer riding momentum tech stocks, which had become skittish. He was losing his discipline and began buying stocks on the way down—averaging down. He needed to get back to his original strategy where he waited for the inflection points. Then, when the stocks would start moving up, he could buy the "fat " part of the pitch.

Lower your daily goal. George was not making the same kind of money as he did before the market turn, and he was getting discouraged. He was shooting for a $100,000 daily goal, but I suggested that he lower that amount to $25,000 a day. This was more doable and would allow him room to build some consistency and success, thus adding to his confidence and helping him regain profits on a more consistent, if smaller, basis.

Reestablish your track record. Chester was down about $700,000. He needed to refocus on reaching his daily goal of $5,000 a day. After a week or two of achieving this goal, he then could move to $15,000 to $20,000 a day. Chester was buying stocks in which he was losing money because he so desperately wanted to trade out of a losing streak. Instead of going for the big bucks right away, he needed to concentrate on his original goal and build a consistent track record again. Then, he could worry about getting bigger.

Follow your established entry points. When Eric moved to a faster paced, shorter-term oriented, catalyst-driven hedge fund, the market was going through this dramatic shift. In the past he was very disciplined in his entry points. He knew when stocks were overvalued and waited longer for stocks to come to him. But during this changing market, he didn't exercise his usual patience and began chasing after stocks. He stopped giving limit orders and was playing a momentum game because he didn't want to miss the moves. He was losing big sums of money. Eric also needed to get back to his usual disciplined game of being more selective and waiting for the right prices before getting into trades.

Continue to do the work. Dale is failing to do the work necessary to make informative trades. He needs to keep doing the analysis he was doing before the market changed. He needs to continue to hold on to his positions when it is justified by his information.

So, if you are having difficulty adapting to a changing market, face the fact that you have gotten off your game and are spending too much time in self-justification, denial, and rationalization. When you are having trouble adjusting, you are focused on the problem. You become defensive and often arrogant rather than being open and looking for what is missing from your trading discipline. Go back to your strategy and use your goal as a valuable lens for examining your trades. In so doing, you may also identify other stubborn, nonproductive attitudes that may be getting in the way of trading in the zone.

Clearing the Hurdles

Psychological obstacles are perhaps the most difficult obstacles of all, because we are in essence battling ourselves. It is never comfortable or easy. If you find yourself repeatedly trapped by the same psychological patterns of thought and behavior, it may be useful to consider the secondary gains or benefits you receive from holding on to them. What do you get from these habits that makes it so difficult to change?

The most simple answer to this question is that thinking and behaving in this way may create an identity or a perspective for you through which to view the world. It also provides a sense of predictability and certainty, but it does so at the cost of mystery, excitement, and the possibility of trading in terms of a larger vision of results and the complete expression of your hidden potential.

Of course, such habits and beliefs have not developed for these secondary gains. But once a defensive pattern is established, it tends to remain, providing a frame of reference for experiencing the world. Only by being aware of how emotionally invested you are in your fixed perspective can you break free from these restrictive habits and become more experientially engaged in your trading.

Chapter 11

Stepping Up to the Challenge

Have you ever met a beginning trader who has struck it big with seemingly little to no effort? He may seem cocky. He may act as if he owns the world. He may think trading is an easy game. Of course, this perception may be because winners are much more vocal than losers. But, with the relative ease in which many get into the field, trading can look deceptively simply, and if you are lucky the first few times, it may not seem as demanding as it is. But trading is really not this way. Repeated trading success involves a lot of elements that don't meet the eye at first, such as hard work, discipline, and the flexibility to keep adapting to continually changing market conditions. To bring all of these ingredients into play, over a sustained period of time ultimately requires the kind of commitment that enables ordinary people to do extraordinary things.

Gaining personal mastery requires a willingness to commit to success because trading most often does *not* provide a quick reward. Committed traders are able to stay in the zone, harnessing the fear, pain, embarrassment, depression, and other negative emotions that interrupt the smooth flow of their trading day. The best traders have to be masters of what the Chinese call active passivity or *wu-wei*. They know how to be patient and how to focus on making the move at the right moment. This capacity for focused attention enables them to identify the best trading opportunities and to capture them in a cost-efficient manner. Remember, mastery is not about buying the right stock. It is about identifying winning trades and maximizing the profitability in these trades and identifying losing trades and minimizing the size of losses in them. The best traders only get it right about 50 percent of the time and make the bulk of their profit in 3 percent to 10 percent of their trades.

Ideally, a master trader is someone who is bright, analytical, self-disciplined, and able to ride out anxiety. He can sell as easily as he can buy. He is able to enjoy a successful performance for the sake of enjoying it, for the sake of really being in the right frame of mind, not just because of the results. When a stock that he has just sold for a profit goes up further, he does not kick himself and bemoan his fate. He examines his success and feels good about it. This characteristic is critical to trading in the zone. He is also able to examine how he could have done better in the trade so that he is better prepared the next time he has a similar opportunity.

Continue the Challenge

Trading in the zone is not just about making money. Someone may earn a lot of money and not feel good. He may be bored. He may experience profitability due to chance or circumstances. Traders need to make the game more interesting. They can't simply rely on old ways of earning money that, even if successful, are not challenging. They need to find new situations, create new objectives, and make sure that they are as fully engaged in the game as they can be.

The most satisfied traders create new challenges—new instruments, new scores, and new financial goals. They expand into new markets. For them, trading is an intellectual challenge, the ability to implement hypotheses and get results. The money is a way of measuring performance and what they have to do to maintain the same level of performance to satisfy investors.

As Mickey, a successful bond trader once told me, "To be in the zone you have to work your ass off, be disciplined, and repeat the trader's mantra, 'Buy well. Sell better.' It's not hard to buy it. It is hard to sell it. You have to be a better seller. It allows you to sleep at night."

Trading is a matter of setting goals, tapping potential, and changing perspectives. In order to remain in the zone, the game has to evolve. You have to raise the bar every chance you get.

"I have to stay positive and poised for the opportunities," said Buster. "I have the radar going, and I am better organizationally. I am in a better mind-set to absorb more. I have to stay in motion."

"Instead of staying at the same level, I need to pyramid things up. After I make 65 percent of what I can make, I ought to start preparing for the next trade. In this way, I can get past 'dead spots.' I can sustain energy and momentum in trade after trade. This preparation will help me to get out of the first trade when it is time, because I already have a 'new baby.' "

"Keep casting for opportunity, and remember there is always a different configuration. You need perspective. You have to be aware of events and what they mean by way of opportunities. It becomes necessary to keep screening for special situations and then to wait for the tug. For example, on April 4, 1999, the finance minister in Sweden resigned. This action probably meant we should have bought the exporters and sold the banks. Somewhere, someone should have started doing the work."

"You have to ask the right questions," said Cameron. "Let go of old habits and start to develop new ones. Most people don't plan six to eight big winners. We don't always make a profit each day, but the work is done each day. The hunt is better than the kill. There is a steady flow of opportunities all through the day. I used to say I was dependent on opportunity. That's not so. I am dependent on finding the opportunity and getting rid of the stuff that is not good."

As Cameron points out, the challenge for the trader is to remain proactive and to keep preparing for new opportunities. The danger for many traders is that they start coasting when they begin to succeed rather than expanding the game further to increase the challenge. You have to keep thinking about the next trade. You have to keep setting up challenging targets and finding new opportunities to meet those targets.

Following are some "Dos" and "Don'ts" that can help you get and stay in the zone. Remember, no matter how successful you are, you can't tread water. You need to step up to the challenge to succeed and then succeed even more.

Do Practice Visual Imagery Rehearsal

By visualizing past positive experiences, you can recreate a mental state of success that will help you as you enter the trading arena. By tapping into the visual, auditory, and kinesthetic memories of past experiences, you can enter into the same winning mind-set you spontaneously experienced when you were on a roll. In this way, you can bring far more confidence and agility to your trades today than you might have without such preparation.

By focusing on positive images, you also can protect yourself from any inclination to dwell too self-critically on yesterday's failures or to become too anxious about the prospects of success today in difficult markets. Visual imagery rehearsal will enhance your alertness and concentration, and you will be better prepared to take measured risks in your trading.

I used this approach with one of the members of the U.S. Olympic bobsled team a number of years ago. He crashed at Zig-zag, a particularly treacherous series of right angle curves midway down the bob-run in Lake Placid, New York. Subsequently, each time he went down, he seemed to unconsciously automatically overcorrect for the previous episode and invariably oversteered the bobsled, either ending up crashing or going too slowly. The speed of the bob-run is so fast that he had very little opportunity in subsequent runs to reprogram himself and free himself from the negative mental images of the first crash.

Although he wasn't consciously afraid, he was unconsciously steering to avoid a crash and paradoxically was crashing more often. I taught him to visualize going down the bob-run in slow motion. I coached him to "steer exactly as if you were coming down the run. Feel the wind. Feel the speed. Feel your muscles tense and shift as you pass the different curves. Steer exactly as you would if you were steering the perfect run. Keep repeating this until you have etched a perfect path in your mind."

He practiced this for thirty minutes making about 100 runs in his mind. When he next went down the run, he was able to steer accurately without having to correct for his earlier crash. He had created a new mental image for steering the course, erasing the negative groove created by the crash.

By rehearsing events in your mind you can develop the steps you will take before you actually enter a particular experience. Then you will be adequately prepared for all possibilities and will have practiced sufficiently so that you are able to master the activity and avoid repeating past mistakes. This exercise applies to a variety of activities from bobsledding to trading.

Remember past successful trades. Tap in the energy of these experiences. If you don't have any, you can make up some positive trades, because the mind ultimately does not distinguish between your memory of a real experience and one you creatively design. You can get power from both. Make up successful stock trades and practice trading successfully. Simulate trades and rehearse different contingencies.

Think about how it feels when things go against you at the end of a trade, or a series of trades, or at the end of the day. Allow yourself to experience the distress, and then practice how to keep focusing on the implementation of your strategy in the face of the discomfort. You can learn to ride out anxious feelings until you experience them as a sense of excitement and are energized by them. Try to rehearse for as many contingencies as possible. Remember, the right thing may not be comfortable, but you can overcome limiting feelings and habits and move forward with excitement and confidence with such preparation.

Jonathan likens this process to his experiences when racing cars. "It's akin to pushing yourself. It's intimidating," he said. "The top 15 guys are close to each other in skill level. So, it's all about ego and bravado. When you pass someone, you need absolute confidence in your ability. If you are timid, you are dead. All the guys are older than I am, and they've been doing it longer. These are people I've looked up to for three or four years. They've taught me a little. But now all of a sudden I've got to beat them. It's psychological. My lap times show I can do it, but I've got to believe it. It's a total mind game. In my mind's eye, I can't as yet see myself passing certain guys. I can't see myself beating them."

In order to pass these guys on the track, Jonathan has to be able to visualize it first. If he doesn't see it, it is not going to happen.

Visualization works the same with trading. In order to press the mark and go past fears and inhibitions, a trader can mentally practice making successful trades until there are no impediments or obstacles. With practice, she can learn to get past any thoughts that stand in the way of her performance. If she can practice doing it in her mind, she will successfully be able to carry through on her planned strategy and reach her goal. And, I cannot emphasize enough, that all of this must be done in conjunction with the preparation, thoughtfulness, and effort involved in processing a lot of information about the companies being traded, market conditions, and other factors discussed throughout this book.

Do Go Further

In order to trade in the zone, you have to be committed, which means you have to constantly be willing to go further than you think you can go. This means being prepared to go past your stopping points—all the psychological inhibitions or limits that you impose on yourself that can keep you from reaching your fullest potential. If identified, these roadblocks can become leverage points for moving into the zone.

So, how do you find the stopping points that can become the cutting edge for change? You do it by reviewing your trades and asking yourself a series of tough questions that will help to identify where you have stopped or where you have veered from your strategy. Since this exercise is tough to do and is critical for trading in the zone, it is often useful to do it with a trading coach, partner, or associate who is willing to help you face the truth about yourself and your trading. The three most critical things to consider are:

- *What is missing?* What dropped out of your trading discipline that has helped you in the past? Did you stop making calls, preparing the night before, or meeting with analysts? Did you stop estimating the risk/reward of your trades or fail to use stops in your trading?

- *What more can you do to maximize your performance?* For example, have you considered keeping a diary of your trades so that you can review them at the end of the day? Or perhaps you should find a trading partner or coach to assist you over any hurdles.

- *Where are you stopped?* Are you paralyzed by the tape action? Are your shorts being squeezed? Have you stopped being nimble in moving in and out of trades? Are you reluctant to take profits? Are you stubbornly trading S&P [Standard & Poor's] futures to make a big killing at what appears to be minimal risk, or trading high flying stocks that you know little about rather than putting your resources into trades where you are really knowledgeable about the companies?

Review your unsuccessful trades with an experienced trader to see what is missing or what else could have been done. Look at your successes to determine what you did that you weren't doing before. To trade in the zone, you have to consider what you must keep doing to reach the objective you have set for yourself.

While all traders say that they want to succeed, they often lack specifically defined goals and a strategy for reaching them. Without goals, it is easy to give in to the notion that they are at the mercy of the markets and that "the markets just aren't cooperating." They are accustomed to living and trading in the realm of predictability, tradition, and reasonableness—rather than in terms of creating miracles or things that didn't exist before by setting stretch targets and committing themselves to reaching them.

It is easy to justify not reaching an outsized goal because to produce extraordinary results or miracles takes commitment, discipline, and a willingness to face the truth about yourself and your trading. It requires a willingness to examine what each day takes in terms of work and focus to realize the goal you have set for yourself. The work required to achieve your goal is often not too far from what you are already doing, but it is doing it with greater consciousness and a willingness to go for it and not be afraid of what might happen if you don't realize your goal.

You *can* produce something that didn't exist before. Maybe it is in the last five minutes, in the last mile, in the last daily efforts where you can really push past the conventional limits—where you can do the extraordinary. To trade in the zone, which is what commitment is about, ultimately requires that you find where the resistance is coming from and break through the everyday notions of complacency. You can achieve this breakthrough by consciously committing to a specific result and then being willing to take the necessary steps consistent with the result in order to bring it about.

> *Case Study*
> "Often, it has to do with the way in which the trader has been raised," said Toby, a shy, introspective trader. He is a nonaggressive trader whose statistics revealed that the bulk of his trades were being done by the DOT [designated order turnaround] machine, an electronic execution system, rather than through floor or upstairs brokers. Trading on the DOT was in fact a form of hiding out for Toby, a stopping point that was keeping him from being as fully engaged in his trading as possible.
>
> Toby needed to take responsibility for his own results. He needed to be more aggressive in his trading. And he also needed to start talking to floor and upstairs brokers. After much coaxing, Toby learned to do both. He learned to speak his mind, to communicate to others what it was that he wanted, and to build relationships that could help him succeed.

Like Toby, when you push yourself way past where you are accustomed to functioning and go beyond the familiar, then something incredible is likely to happen. What more can you do that will get you to your goal? Consider:

- Who else you can call.

- What you can do outside your usual routine to increase your performance.

- What you can get from going outside your way of seeing things, by stretching beyond what is conventional.

If someone is hard to call, then he is the guy to call. Doing things in the customary way isn't the answer. If you are committed to reaching your goal, do what you have to do, especially if it is uncomfortable.

Of course, as we discuss in Chapter 7, there are times when there are no opportunities, and you are better off staying on the sidelines. Then you don't want to press too hard. Trading out of boredom is a recipe for disaster.

In addition, there are also going to be successful trades in which you still could have made more. But you must learn to be satisfied with those successes as such because, given the information at the time, you traded them well. You can't get too frustrated with winners that did the unexpected and then went even further. Enjoy the good trades and learn to make more good trades. Remember the good feeling associated with those trades and "fight like the devil to avoid losing that feeling."

"To be in the zone, you have to be able to examine your successes and feel good about them," said Jim. "Examine how they could have been better, but feel good about them too."

Success in trading is more like running a marathon than running a sprint, and you have to keep working at it to tap more of your hidden potential.

For example, in marathon training you may hit the wall at 18 miles, but beyond that you may experience a second burst of energy that gives you new momentum. In some way, the race begins toward the end. Often, you are able to get past the last hurdles, but you will not know unless you persevere that far. Pushing beyond your limits requires motivation and determination. In reality, you don't know how far you can go. As you overcome hurdles along the way, you create new openings for opportunities hitherto undreamed of.

Do Focus

In the face of distraction, it is easy to lose sight of the major tasks. When you don't stay focused, you can soon find yourself in a vicious cycle of losing, rationalizing, and blaming other things for your difficulties. Although it is difficult to do, it is also imperative at this point to take a moment to regroup and reassess where you are and to begin to focus once again on what must be done.

"In the last two weeks, I lost the focus I had," said Jordan. "Part of it is because of my transition into a new group. I am learning new stuff, but I have to stay conscious all the time. I have gotten casual before. For example, I always lose money when the boss from London is in town. I am too busy making up excuses instead of focusing."

"I played against this guy in basketball, and he beat me," he continued. "By the third and fourth game he was getting sloppy. I have done that with my trading too. I have been in his position and deteriorated because of overconfidence."

It is critical to be in a game-readiness mode all the time. If you pay attention, there are rewards. Stay conscious, centered, and concentrated, and the possibilities are unlimited.

However, staying focused does not mean doing only one thing at a time. On the contrary, another characteristic of being in the zone is the ability to concentrate on a number of things at once. This skill can be developed by learning to concentrate on one thing at a time and then adding additional things. You should learn to function at many tasks—following stocks while you are talking on the telephone and listening to the room for shouts of new opportunities. You should be able to pay attention to a number of stocks at the same time so that you can keep reviewing your portfolio and interpreting the meaning of the data as it comes through.

Case Studies

Dick is a master trader who is way ahead of the curve in processing information. He builds nonlinear relationships in his head. He is always looking for the relationships between events in one sector and the implications in other stocks and other sectors. If something is going on in oil stocks, for example, he is trying to understand the implications not only for oil drillers but for airlines and railroads and perhaps consumer products that may reflect consumer spending patterns.

He also efficiently compartmentalizes a great amount of information and keeps his focus for long periods of time without being easily influenced by the opinions of others. He is constantly reviewing his positions, upgrading his theses with new information, and moving in and out of positions in a flexible fashion so as to reduce his risk and maximize his profitability. He is dedicated to the process of trading in the zone more than anything else and does not become attached to his theories about the stocks he trades or the movements of the markets. In this way he garners as much value from his trades as he can. He is always prepared, always in the now.

By contrast, Ben had a problem with losing focus because when things weren't going well he would start thinking about the past, become self-critical and negative, and lose the flexibility needed for trading in the zone. The key for Ben and many other traders is to find ways of getting into a positive, proactive state of mind so that they can enjoy what they are doing, take profits when they are available, and get out of losing positions so that they can reallocate their money to winning opportunities.

"Now, I am taking a more proactive approach," he said. "I am focusing in a more conscious way on defining catalysts, delegating responsibility for making calls, reducing the size of my portfolio, and taking bigger positions in the stocks I have when they are working."

Ben was willing to explore what he needs to do to get to the next level of play in terms of consistency, digging in, making the calls, and pressing his team. He needs to be encouraged to get to the next level and not merely assume that he is a star who will naturally get there. For example, he decided not to hold on to certain stocks just to be in the market and sold those in which he didn't have an edge.

Staying focused means preparing and moving slowly forward with a vision for the future without impulsiveness. It also means prioritizing information and activities so that you can also find other sources of satisfaction in life.

Don't Abandon Your Opinion

In order to maintain the motivation you need to push the limits of your trading, you have to resist the inclination to relinquish your own opinions. When you defer to the opinions of others, you give up your own beliefs. Then, when you lose, you may feel especially embarrassed and start trading defensively to recover your public persona or image.

When you trade this way, you tend to focus on not losing money so as not to look foolish or are trying to get a big hit in order to look good. In doing so, you take yourself out of your disciplined game, creating more insecurity and more effort to trade to look good. You are in a vicious cycle of trading to protect your ego not trading in the zone.

Case Study
Computer- and Internet-related stocks boomed in 1999. Pat was an analyst-turned-trader who was very familiar with this group. He noted that many of the largest gains had come in stocks with barely any earnings but with the high expectations that they would succeed in the Internet-related economy of the future. He was fully cognizant of the fact that many of these Internet-related stocks were overvalued. At the same time companies like Cisco, Dell, Microsoft, and others had substantial growth and did indeed provide support and justification for high evaluations. Pat bought 17,000 shares of one large tech stock at $100 per share. This was a big position for him to take.

"The print didn't work. It went sour from the word 'go.' It was down on the opening. I held on to it. That day it was down $1 or $2," he said. "There were good reasons to buy it. Technology was going through the roof. This print cleaned up a big seller. But sure enough, it was a bogus print. We got hooked by the brokerage firm."

"I should have sold it, but four other people in the room were also in it. The consensus was to hold on to it. That was Friday. Monday we came in, and the tech stock was buying another company. The stock was down $9. It was the biggest one-day decline in its history, and I just bought my largest position in it. I sold it, and that morning it popped up three points from the open. It is costing me my month. Meanwhile, I made a bunch of trading mistakes because I was preoccupied with the loss."

Pat should have stuck with his discipline and gotten rid of the stock when he knew the trade was bad. In addition, he shouldn't have allowed himself to get distracted by this trade, which caused him to make mistakes in other trades. You can't try to get back losses by trading wildly nor should you let one set of trades distort the way you trade other positions. You have to compartmentalize the losing trades and go back to following your basic strategy. Pat actually admitted to being off his game from the "get-go" with this tech stock. He just wanted to trade "with the other guys."

In fact, Pat frequently allowed himself to be talked out of his trades. He often failed to evaluate his information and bought into the dogmatic views of others. Instead, he needed to qualify and evaluate the opinions of others, challenge them, and challenge himself to see what the reasons for the trade were. He needed to do the work, follow his conviction, and play his own game.

Don't Say "Burnt Out"

When a trader starts to lose, the tendency sometimes is to explain the phenomenon as burnout. Classifying a losing streak or a trading slump in this way tends to make an event out of it. Then traders begin to associate their losses with other events or emotions such as turning 40, running out of steam, or the changing nature of the markets.

Although the explanations may seem valid, it is precisely this type of self-critical, judgmental thinking that is the problem, not the specific stress factor. When a trader looks for excuses for why he is losing, he is already out of the zone and off his strategy.

This type of self-flagellation also may lead to unproductive comparisons, where you notice younger or less successful traders doing better than you are and can't explain it. This repetitive negative thinking will only magnify your sense of losing power and may lead to maladaptive efforts to bolster yourself psychologically. These efforts may take a variety of forms, from compulsive efforts to recoup all of your losses in a few big high risk bets where you start trading stocks you don't really know, to avoidance and withdrawal from trading so that you don't end up with a loss.

To move beyond your limits and truly trade in the zone, you must be able to stand outside of yourself and see that you are putting yourself down, making conclusive statements about your losing ability, and looking for excuses.

"Trading is an act of courage," said Lou. "It is critical to keep your perspective and not lose heart when everyone around you is losing confidence."

Traders who find themselves in such a losing slump may want to do one or more of the following:

- Consider the facts. Examine their profit and loss (P&L).
- Reduce the burdens they are placing on themselves.
- Become more self-reliant.
- Relinquish an excessive sense of responsibility for others.
- Consider their own interests more carefully.
- Do not allow themselves to be judged by others' standards.

The critical issue is to see that you are caught in a self-fulfilling failure chain that must be recognized for what it is. Notice your efforts to gain reassurance. Realign your focus on your goal (not your losses), and move forward with an intentional plan.

Don't Withdraw

There is a difference between rest and withdrawal, and it is a vital point for the trader to understand. Rest is defined as a bodily state of minimal function and metabolic activity. It is a time to gain a peace of mind through the ceasing of action and to gain a freedom from anxiety or disturbance. Therefore, by taking a break and resting, you can temporarily stop yourself, regroup, and begin trading again in a more successful and determined way.

Withdrawal, however, is defined as backing away or turning away from the object of attention. It involves moving out of a place or position. It means you have left the game. When you withdraw, you are no longer an active participant. You are no longer focusing or absorbing information. You have quit at some level.

When a trader withdraws from trading, he is taking his eyes not only off his trades, but essentially off his goal. He is not using the time as a period of reflection to see what he can do better. Instead, he is retreating because of fear, frustration, or some other unidentified emotion.

Establishing a stretch target enables you to get past fear and frustration, bypass your inhibitions and habits, and find more creative ways to trade in the zone. Pursuing such an objective helps you to modify your behavior and to move away from limiting self-concepts. But remember defining a specific target isn't easy to do. It requires effort and doesn't work immediately. You will need to be patient when you don't reach your goals quickly and not get discouraged when your actions don't seem to bring you any closer to your objectives.

It's even worse if you experience a series of losses. Then, it is easy to fall back into old habits or completely back away from the game. Just as the body's inflammatory response may be more problematic than the invasion of bacteria, the response to a disaster may be more problematic than a loss itself when the trader's response is to withdraw from the game.

"I got out to avoid losses," said Jonathan. "Then, I realized that I have to keep looking where to buy again and get back in the game. I see the value of being able to come in and trade. I have to be in the game. I don't need to withdraw. Being in the game is what it is about. It hurts if you lose, but it is all about being in the game."

As discussed throughout this book, losing is simply part of the process. Being in the game is the life-affirming activity. But, it is also essential to understand that traders, like most professionals, may, at some point in their careers, need to take a temporary rest from the game. They may need to set aside a time to recoup in order to get back on line with their strategy and to begin trading in the zone once more.

For example, the beginning trader has few positive experiences to allow him to sustain a succession of losses. As one loss is compounded by another loss, he may lose confidence rapidly. He then begins each day not with a fresh view but with the burden of trying to recapture all he has lost. He becomes overwhelmed by an excessive target and unable to trade with the focus he needs. Soon, he may face total paralysis and an empty feeling in the pit of his stomach that he is in the wrong profession.

The only remedy then is to temporarily rest and recover and come back with a smaller, manageable objective and a willingness to trade one or two stocks for a minimum amount of profit. As he builds confidence in his ability to steadily produce consistent results, he can then progress to the next rung of the ladder.

"I was too focused on the give back and appearances, not on playing the game. I had lost track of my vision. Then, I realized I had to stop trying to save myself and protect my image," said Jonathan. "I shifted back into the game. All you have is the dream, the capacity to look beyond the situation you are in."

Remember: Rest, maybe. Withdraw, never!

Take the Step

In order to reach the zone, you have to be in the game. You have to let your objective govern what you do. And you have to go beyond today's limitations. Reach today's potential and learn to expand your potential through focus, research, and trading technique improvement—a little every day.

Although this process is not easy, it is a necessary one. If you limit yourself to only what you "think" you can do, you will never truly reach the fullness of your potential, and that is what trading in the zone is all about.

The market goes up. The market goes down. The markets may be tough, but the best players seem to do well, no matter what the market is. To get yourself psyched up, in the same sense that an athlete has to prepare for his or her big event, the trader has to get his or her mind on the game and get rid of negative thoughts.

The great traders are able to identify their own self-sabotaging patterns and work to eradicate them. One trader described a master trader in this way:

"The person who trades in the zone learns to be brave to the point where he no longer has to think about it. He is comfortable enough that he can regularly confront uncertainty, recover rapidly from loss, and empower his associates to stretch their horizons. He processes information rapidly and translates it into action. He compartmentalizes losses and shifts nimbly as markets reverse. He is also disciplined in knowing when to exit a trade."

Of course, all of this information applies to bond traders as well as equity traders.

"All the principles discussed here in terms of trading in the zone apply to bond traders as well as equity traders," said Jim, another bond trader. "Bonds are not different. The philosophies are the same. It is discipline, expertise, an intense work ethic, and a love for what you do. This allows you to get into the zone and stay in it."

Great traders are born, but really good ones can be made. Discipline can be learned. From discipline comes self-confidence, the ability to handle difficult situations, and control over your own emotions and actions amidst the uncertainty of the trading markets. You can do it too. You *can* step up to the challenge and trade in the zone.

Part Five

Using Advanced Strategies

Chapter 12

Taking Advantage of Capitulation

What's fascinating about many great athletes is that as they mature they don't just get better at their specialty. They multiply their skills and actually add new elements to their game. For example, a baseball player who has a great fastball adds a split-finger fastball to his repertoire. The tennis champ with a cannonball serve works on a nasty slice second serve as well. In the same vein, traders—especially master traders—keep enhancing and multiplying their skills.

You may not realize it yet, but once you begin to trade in the zone, you too will gain the momentum to grow in ways you might never have imagined. Trading in the zone enables you to do a number of things well. You can trade size, manage losses better, keep moving, process more information, and act more decisively on it. You can get a better feel for the price action and have a good head for a story. Most of all, trading in the zone lets you eventually step up to a new level of trading, putting into action the most advanced counterintuitive strategies such as is most dramatically illustrated in mastering capitulation trades and short selling.

Advanced strategies should only be pursued after you have become proficient at the more basic strategies in this book and *Trading to*

Win. Only when you have mastered these trading disciplines can you begin to do the more complex counterintuitive trades, where you seem to go against the grain of what a proper trading strategy ought to be, but you are doing it for specific, goal-oriented reasons.

Defining Capitulation

Capitulation is one of the most psychologically driven events in the market. It is the result of the emotional buying or selling that creates price extremes at either high or low levels. Although capitulation is a complicated phenomenon that can occur for a variety of reasons, it offers the advanced trader a unique opportunity to put all of the principles outlined in this book into a series of counterintuitive trading moves that are often extremely profitable. Traders rarely differentiate between capitulation tops and bottoms because the psychological underpinnings are very similar in both instances, but it is useful to understand the distinctions between the two types of capitulation events.

Capitulation on the Upside

A capitulation on the upside is a capitulation of the shorts. Otherwise known as a capitulation top, it happens when those who have been shorting a stock are being squeezed by the advancing price of the stock caused by frenzied buying and extreme optimism to levels that are no longer sustainable. The shorts are losing money as the price moves up, pushed up by buyers who have to own the stock and are willing to pay up for it and the fact that there may not be enough sellers around. Fearful of an ever-increasing price, the sellers become so frightened that the elevation in prices will never cease that they panic and experience enormous pressure to cover their positions and buy back the stock. With a shortage of stock, the price goes even higher, reaching what is known as a blow-off top where the price goes way beyond expectations until the buyers become sellers of the stock.

Often capitulation is started by the short sellers panicking to cover. In effect, they take the rally higher. Once they cover their positions and run the stock price up farther, they run out of gas. Then another short seller comes in.

The onset of capitulation is marked by a blow-off. Blow-offs are price action moves of stocks where they explode or dramatically move upward to levels beyond what might be expected. Essentially blow-offs mark inflection points driven by changes in fundamentals. The trader who can remain cool, calm, and collected and follow the price action without picking up the panic of the crowd can take advantage of these situations to short a stock before the blow-off and then prepare to buy the stock back after panic selling forces everything down.

Case Study
Dominick shorted a major communication company that had run up to dizzying heights in anticipation of a red hot IPO of an innovative subsidiary. The stock went from 70 to 130 in a week. Most traders who were shorting the company initially held on to their short positions believing that the high valuations were absurd. Sandy, believing that it was wildly overvalued, waited until the short sellers could no longer tolerate the pain as the price of the stock rose on the day of the spin-off. As the subsidiary opening indications continued to climb (ascribing even higher values to the parent company), the pain of the shorts increased. Dominick implemented his shorts as the other shorts were forced out. Then he waited for the stock to drop and began getting ready to buy it once it had come down.

To take advantage of this type of capitulation, a trader needs to remain focused and prepared to act without responding to the market sentiment at the time of the event. For his timing to be impeccable, he needs to be able to trade in the zone. According to one successful trader: "This is the hardest thing for a human being to manage. Just imagine buying when the rest of the world is selling."

Capitulation on the Downside
Capitulation on the downside is a capitulation of the longs who bought stock, only to find that instead of going up, the stock is going down. They buy more as the price drops with the intention of averaging down, but this action only digs them deeper into the hole.

As the stock starts to bottom, the capitulation occurs and traders who are long panic and sell. They feel it is the end of the world and that the stock is going to zero. They want out at any cost. They can't tolerate the discomfort and race to get out of losing positions. This massive sell-off kills the price of the stock, but at this point the traders no longer care about the price. At the low, a big buyer usually appears and takes out all these panicky sellers of stock, which pushes the stock price up again. At the bottom, as sellers get out of their positions and eventually disappear, the selling dissipates, and the stock has nowhere to go but up.

"A capitulation low happens when the market moves against a very big position that needs to be liquidated," one trader explained. "Say I'm long a stock at 10. It goes to 8, then to 7, then to 3. I am thinking 'What should I do?' Meanwhile, it goes to 2, and I panic. I sell down to 1. That's the capitulation—the panic. If I were trading in the zone, like a master trader I would be able to buy the stock at 1, and, when it goes up to 3, sell it and take a profit. To be able to buy after the capitulation bottom requires the ability to move against the crowd. This takes courage and discipline because you are taking a shot at something that everyone else has decided is worthless."

Case Study
On April 4, 2000, the Dow Jones industrial average and the Nasdaq dropped significantly before rallying back dramatically. The decline was so sudden and fast that thousands of margin calls went out throughout the country, and many trading accounts were shut down. Many new investors saw their recently acquired wealth disappear in a flash, and many seasoned traders were seriously shaken.

In the same day, the market had one of its biggest single-day declines and one of its biggest single day recoveries. At 1:18 P.M., the Nasdaq Composite Index was down 574.57 points or 13.6 percent as a result of panic selling. When the selling finally stopped, the index had recovered 451.84 points in a little more than one hour. By the end of the day the Nasdaq was at 4148.89, which was down 74.79—only 1.77 percent.

The Dow Jones average was also affected by the panic selling. The sell-off was in part attributable to some traders selling Dow industrial stocks to obtain the cash needed to meet the margin calls on Nasdaq stocks. The sell-off continued in the afternoon, after the Standard & Poor's (S&P) futures fell in price and caused another wave of selling.

The drop had followed a one and a half year run up in New Economy stocks like the Internet stocks, very low evaluations for the Old Economy stocks, and a three week effort to correct this since March 10, 2000 (the day the Nasdaq number had reached its peak of 5,048.62). From March 10 to April 5 that index had dropped 17.8 percent to 4,169.21. Over that same period, the Dow had risen 1.1 percent with solid gains in many blue chip stocks.

While there were many explanations for this shift, what interests us is that the dramatic drop represented the most volatile day ever in the stock market and one of the best opportunities for master traders to take advantage of what amounted to a massive market capitulation.

Trading in a Collapsing Market

Although trading in response to dramatic events in the market takes good instincts and experience, it can be learned. Indeed, trading in the zone basically should prepare you to trade even when the market is collapsing and it is extremely difficult psychologically to trade.

When any dramatic move begins to take place, investors tend to follow the herd—either panic selling or impulsively buying. In addition, the more extreme the market move, the greater the pressure is to follow the crowd. It takes a conscious effort to steer clear of the herd mentality that often takes over when markets become volatile.

The master trader gets involved in the trading in order to get a feel for the market, how easy or difficult it is to make trades, and to determine why sellers are pulling their offers. Are they doing it in order to get a better price, or are there are no bids from buyers? The latter answer suggests several things:

- The market is starting to drop.
- Liquidity is drying up.
- The trader with excessively large positions may be stymied and unable to get out.

On April 12, 13, and 14, skilled traders got defensive and took their positions down. They took note of the dry-up of liquidity and the major downturn in the market and then took action in advance of the market decline so they wouldn't be hurt by it. They were sensitive to the maximum point of pain and were alert enough to recognize the inflection points in selected stocks, sectors, or the market as a whole. By trading in the zone, the master trader was able to stay calm and to sell during the panic buying of the shorts who had been squeezed and/or was able to buy when the market was collapsing and the longs were pressured to sell near the bottom. The critical thing is that he was able to read the market responses and able to resist the pressure to which everyone else was falling prey. The master trader is, in fact, attuned to the emotionality in the marketplace and the people around him and is able to stay focused on his own decisions and not pressed by the force of events into less than optimal decision making. In a word, he is able to keep moving.

In order to take advantage of a capitulation, you have to overcome the obvious. You have to move to a higher plane. You have to harness your fear and allow it to take you to another level. You cannot make your decisions based on your opinions or feelings because, like a magnet, you will instinctively be drawn to the philosophies and fears of the majority. In effect, to trade capitulation moves successfully requires you to master your own emotions and to trade in the zone.

For these reasons, Marcus talks about capturing the capitulation event as the Holy Grail of trading, the ultimate step in mastery. You make decisions based on objective observations, not how you feel or how the group is feeling.

"These events occur on days when the market looks like it is going to zero. People are panicking because there are no bids for stocks. The more people panic, the more panic is created on the street. The sellers stop selling, and the people that weren't buying start buying them again. No one wants to stand out there by themselves," he said. "If you are willing to stand out there by yourself, you are the hero."

In the face of a capitulation, you have to employ all of the lessons outlined in this book. You have to use your emotions to your advantage and not be controlled by them. You have to notice your distress and the distress of others and trade independently of these feelings.

Managing an Inflection

When an important level is broken and the market starts to trade wide gaps, which is reflective of strong emotion, and everyone is freaking out, you have to use your adrenaline response constructively.

You assess the dynamics of the trade, in particular by looking at the supply and demand. You try to understand when it's a real story. Sometimes there is money to be made on the price action. Sometimes it is driven by perception. You trade the market *movement*, not on opinion or emotion. You commit to the result, which brings you to a higher level of consciousness about your trading. You have to be more conscious more of the time than most traders.

The reasons for a capitulation can vary and may not always be completely evident. Some traders may feel it occurred for one reason. Others may see it as a result of something totally different.

For example, some traders thought the April 4 capitulation was a result of a shift in investor psychology and a shift toward reevaluating the new high-flying companies. Some blamed a prominent Wall Street analyst for recommending that her company's clients scale back their technology holdings. Others attributed the decline to the collapse of settlement negotiations between Microsoft and the government. As noted previously, on April 4, 2000, a number of traders felt the panic was a result of the large number of sudden margin calls. These market calls were a result of the large amount of debt incurred in buying more risky New Economy Internet stocks. Therefore, it is useful to understand the nature of the business models that are being developed by some of the new companies so as to be sensitive to the kinds of issues that will impact on their profitability and their price in the market place.

Regardless of the reasons, there are some specific macro events that traders can look for in determining whether a capitulation is imminent. Often some of the following situations combined with negative sentiment create the setting for a capitulation of buyers or sellers:

- The weakening of the dollar.
- Tightening by the Fed.
- A strengthening of the Euro and yen.
- A large trade deficit, or a shortfall of earnings by a significant company.
- The imminent resurgence of bonds that may have been down for months.

Once traders recognize that a capitulation is imminent or occurring, they still have to notice and work through their own emotions in order to take advantage of it. The master trader has to be aware of the mood of the crowd and cannot let his own emotional responses color his decisions as they pertain to taking advantage of the movement of the crowd.

Most battles are won because of preparation. Most soldiers train for events, and how well they do depends on preparation. The same applies to trading. The best traders develop an uncanny ability to read the Street, price action, volume, and panic. In effect, the master trader understands the need to prepare in advance, to have alternative plans, and then commit to action in a very short time. He has to be willing to play.

The master trader buys the stock as it starts to move in his favor and starts selling when the tide turns against him. He waits until others are fatigued by the price action and uncertain as to where the stock is heading. He watches the general market indices for rallies and confirmation and trades based on fact, not feeling. Other traders will not have the confidence to play, but he sees just how psychologically fatigued they get. This helps him make his decision to buy as it is going up, when everyone else is reluctant to buy because of the high price or when it is too low after the capitulation on the bottom when everyone else has lost belief in the possibility of a win. In order to manage the capitulation, the master trader is always reading the mood of the crowd and taking advantage of his own coolness to trade in terms of these psychologically driven movements.

The problem with capitulation is that people see stocks spiking down and buy 50 more. "I've learned not to panic when the market is down," Dominick said. "I don't have to worry about it gapping down. It is a real company. It will average down. Once I get there, I will be at a point of maximum liquidity and inflection. I am dealing with it while the fire is happening."

Capitulation is the major psychological strategy of the master trader. While many traders hesitate to pursue this strategy for fear that there may be the start of a crash, the master trader remains objective, refusing to believe that the world is coming to an end, again. He has been there before. The best traders are willing to go against the crowd. This is confidence.

Can you learn to do this? Yes.

According to Al: "You can measure the anxiety of a group of traders. Watch the faces of the traders in the room when they all look scared. Look to see if they are in pain. If they were buyers of stocks, they would have bought them at a certain level. When the stock breaks below the support level, they are losing money. That's when they start to feel pain. If you bought World Com at $12 before it split 42 times, you are not going to freak out if it goes down to $50. But if something had been going up and is now losing money, people are not having a good time."

"When it comes to money, people will do anything to make it and anything not to lose it," he continued. "When the market fails after it has been successful, it hurts people a lot more."

Of course, a loss is a loss, and a failure after a big success is only painful because of greed. Fear and greed are equivalents. As you approach irrational behavior, whether exuberance or fear, you get to the extreme of human emotion. The presence of such behavior is usually the best contraindicator.

What makes the master trader so unique is that he trades counterintuitively. He sells into rallies and buys the dips. This sounds simple to do, but it isn't.

"The hardest thing to do is not so much being right by picking the right stocks, but being able to take the profit when I have made a lot of money, instead of holding on trying to make more money out of greed and ending up losing a lot of my profit," said Jordan. "The worst trades have been when I was up a half million in a stock and didn't sell and take some profit. It requires a huge amount of discipline to do that."

While the market swings up and down, trading in the zone allows you to remain calm—not euphoric at the top and not depressed at the bottom. Because of his expertise at handling his own emotions and reading the face of the market, the master trader can trade successfully when others are just flailing about.

Chapter 13

Short Selling

"It ain't easy being green," sang Kermit, the most famous frog in the universe. In the universe of day traders—especially in the midst of a bull market where the natural bias is to the upside—it ain't easy being a short seller. You've got to be comfortable enough in your own skin to act on your shorts, when everyone around you is long. The ability to short stocks, which takes a higher level of conviction to execute, is an art form in its own right, and the act of short selling is not mastered by many. Even professional traders have difficulty betting against a rising stock, and that is exactly what short sellers do.

Basically, short selling is the reverse of a long trade. Typically, a trader buys a stock, hopes the price will rise, and then sells to make a profit. But a short seller "borrows" a stock from someone who owns it, sells it, and hopes the price goes down. Then he can buy the stock back at a lower price, "return" the stock to its owner, and pocket the profit.

Except where shorting is done as a hedge in order to mute volatility in a long short portfolio, "and provide insurance should the market go down instead of up, " short selling can be much riskier than a typical long trade where the amount of loss is limited to the amount paid for the stock. A trader cannot lose more than he paid for the stock, but his potential profit is unlimited. In a short, however, the trader's profit potential is not greater than the dollar value of the stock going to $0, but his loss could be infinite. What makes matters even more complicated is that the stock's owner can demand the stock back at any time, and the trader has to return it—no matter where the price currently stands.

To succeed at short selling, you must be able to do many of the things discussed in this book to an even larger degree than those performing typical long trades. The short seller must trade against the generally bullish context in which most trading occurs because of what appears to be the natural tendency of most traders to want to buy, the fact that most institutions and mutual funds are both predisposed and often restricted to only buying securities, and the inherently long bias of the "sell side" brokerage firms on Wall Street. To sell short successfully in the face of this bias toward the long side, and often against prevailing sentiment, takes discipline, focus, and a lot of fundamental work.

Developing a Thesis

What is important to the short seller? How does he look at a company? What is he trying to do? The short seller is trying to identify issues facing a company or the industry as a whole that will make a stock go down. He is looking for fundamental flaws in the business and is attuned to negative news, innuendo, and other subtle and concrete signs that indicate that things aren't what they appear to be and that something could go wrong.

To prove the consensus wrong, the short seller often starts by questioning the assumptions that go into the company's earnings and Street estimates. Do they reflect reality? What are the real and relative values of a company, and what information does this value encapsulate?

"The essential work that you must do, if you want to be a short seller, is to find structural weaknesses in problem companies where there is an 80 percent downside probability that the stock will drop," said Al, who was known for his ability to find short opportunities. "I generally look for stocks that can drop 25 percent to 80 percent in value."

"When I am developing a thesis on a possible short, I look for accounting problems, pending mergers (to hide problems), and other problematic factors. Once I have a general thought process, I then pay close attention to price and volume technical patterns, which tell me when a stock is about to enter the one- to three-month period of its greatest decline. I look for good companies whose shares are very overvalued or not factoring in some real problems. I also am looking for issues that might cause a contraction in the high multiples that a company may be trading at. Essentially, I am looking for overvalued companies that will prove disappointing in the near future. I look for inflection points, which are benchmarks and clues, such as:

- Insider sales.

- A company that is avoiding questions and not returning calls.

- A large merger that is being used to obscure slowing growth prospects.

- Weak sectors.

- Inventory that is growing faster than sales.

- A company that recently prereleased that the earnings would 'be in line' but curiously did not give the revenue line.

- Comps going from solid double digits to mid-single digits.

- A company that has indicated that they will sacrifice gross margin for higher sales."

Short sellers incorporate many factors such as macroeconomic data, company-specific information, and clearly defined events to form an educated hypothesis about a stock's performance. Even though a trader is trading on a short-term basis, he is still concerned about structural and industrial issues as well as sales and accounting numbers. He does not simply rely on price action movement nor on general notions about the company, but on highly specific details which are then subjected to a careful thought process. More importantly, by focusing on specific dates, the trader can provide himself with a benchmark or time frame in which to see if his conclusions are borne out or accepted by the market. The trader is on the lookout for any signs that his view will soon be embraced. Serious traders also approach the market with multiple options so they can be prepared to get out of the position if the thought process or premise is unclear or proved wrong.

"It is easier to short a stock when you have a view," said Al. "Then you can withstand the pain better. Psychologically, you have to be able to ride out the discomfort when your hypothesis doesn't initially work out. The thesis provides a basis for differentiating between random and real market movement. The thesis helps you to notice when you are wrong. This isn't always easy."

The biggest problem for the short seller is to lose his objectivity. "If you become too firm in your views and don't respect the volatility, you can be hurt," continued Al. "You can't be locked into your game plan. You have to know which plays to follow as they pan out or don't pan out. For example, if there is a meeting and it doesn't go as you expected, then you have to consider whether you should reconsider your position. To do so you need several scenarios, a thought process which is likely to change as both the price and information about a stock changes."

Defining a Good Short

There are several types of shorts and each one requires an understanding of a different aspect of information. Some are based on understanding the structural weaknesses of the company; others are based on perception or understanding false perceptions on the street. Let's examine five different types of shorts:

1. *Macro shorts.* For example, a previously optimistic perception of a new technology has changed (e.g., in the dot.coms), or the economy has slowed and people are spending less.

2. *Micro shorts.* You are short based on something specific about another company. For example, a retailer misses a quarter and you look to short the largest supplier to the retailer.

3. *Perception shorts.* No matter how good the numbers are, the stock is still going down. The perception of a weakening company may be wrong, but it is still affecting the trade. The

company's fundamentals might be solid, but expectations as reflected in the stock price have reached unsustainable levels. Therefore, there is an opportunity to short. This is an example of the Wall Street shibboleth: "Buy the rumor. Sell the news."

4. *Fundamental shorts.* There is a fundamental or structural weakness in the company.

5. *Supply versus demand shorts.* When there are artificial imbalances among stocks, for example, you can short the new stocks being added to an index that are likely to go up artificially and temporarily on the day they are added to the index. At the same time, you can go long on the index itself, which may initially drop at the time of the addition of the new stocks.

According to Gary, another experienced short seller: "The short seller looks for a balance between anecdotes and hard facts, signs along the way that validate or alter his original thesis. A first consideration is whether the stock is overvalued or something is wrong with the company."

"From a more technical perspective," he continues, "it is useful to consider the way in which the stock has been trading. Ask yourself the following questions:

- Did they run the stocks up artificially at the end of the day?

- Is there relative weakness? Is there a pronounced down trend?

- Is the stock oversold in a bull market? If so, it is likely to do poorly in a bear market, although this statement is not always true as some stocks act in opposition to the overall market.

- Has the stock been going down, and is it now up in a down tape? If so, it is a good stock to short rather than cover.

- Is it a bad stock that had been going down and is now in the middle of a short covering rally where it is up in a down tape?

- Are the stocks losing price momentum or in industries with problems?"

A short seller can look for companies where the fundamentals are peaking and the stocks have discounted all the positive fundamentals and aren't going to get any better. There is probably no positive news flow to come for these stocks and usually that causes the longs to exit their positions, which may occur after a big move up. This same concept gets more complex in companies such as paper, steel, and chemicals, for example, where the underlying commodities are not controlled by the companies and usually dictate the gyrations in the stock price. You can sometimes short good commodity companies when the commodity is going down. Nevertheless, it may be more difficult to short when it is a well-managed and highly diversified company that can sustain growth in diversified businesses and be less affected by drops in commodity prices.

Missed Earnings

Another critical stock selection strategy is to consider missed earnings, which underscore the fact that expectations may have been too high.

When a company misses its publicly guided earnings estimates, because, for example, it may have blown through its budget, the CEO may challenge the operating team to improve the next quarter. The team may start scrambling to improve the bottom line and actually show temporary improvement without necessarily correcting the basic structural inefficiencies.

Missed earnings often trigger panic selling and lead to precipitous price drops and the withdrawal from the marketplace of buyers and sellers who have become price insensitive because the near-term outlook is no longer as favorable as originally expected. Missed earnings are particularly important because companies that missed earnings in the past quarter or past two quarters may do so again. Using this variable as a screen, Ron shorted UVW after it missed earnings in the second and third quarter of 1999 and made 6 points on the downside from 42 to 36.

In effect, looking for broken stocks with missed earnings and disappointed expectations is one way of selecting potentially profitable shorts. The strategy is to short them before the earnings reports. These stocks may drift up and then drop after reporting earnings. The key to shorting is to pick the top when the stock is about to roll over.

Shorting Positives

When all of the upcoming good news about a company is already in the marketplace, it may be a time to short a stock, especially if expectations are too high The best places to look for these shorts are among companies that have promised more than they can deliver.

One trader explained, "There are times when I will short a company after the stock has performed well, and I have identified an upcoming event that people unilaterally expect to be positive. For example, there is a consensus that the earnings will be beaten by 3 cents, the top line will grow 25 percent, the margins will improve 50 basis points, and the company should be splitting its stock 2 for 1. These types of stories have a tendency to move stocks up considerably into an earnings date. But if everyone out there already owns the stock when the news (albeit positive) is released, the only action that investors have to complete their long trades is to sell that stock into the good news."

"Occasionally, you suffer some pain on the short side temporarily, but more often than not these stocks sell off on the good news, making your short a profitable trade. However, if this company only beats the EPS [earnings per share] number by one cent, or if the top line growth is only up 15 percent, or if margins are only up 25 basis points, or if they only announce a 3 for 2 stock split, the market will sell the stock off more sharply because the company (even though still performing well) did not meet expectations. This is where the short seller can make a lot of money."

Case Study
XYZ went from 5 to 21, then to 180. One trader had an analyst who kept advising him to short it. Sandy didn't want to trade it from the long side. He thought the company was ahead of itself. The stock went into the 30s.

"The issues that were relevant at 21 are relevant today at 31," said the trader. "They were relevant all along, but there has been a change in sentiment. Now the company is no longer being highly overvalued based on sentiment. The realization by the Street was that the revenue growth was too optimistic. The issue led to making it a short."

Does the stock reflect the Street's assumptions? Maybe not. Perhaps the Street doesn't understand the strength of the product. The smart short seller doesn't accept the Street's assumptions about business models at face value. He questions the variables that go into the analysis. This contrarian view is essential for successful short selling.

Perfecting the Timing and Relevance

The master short seller not only seeks to make an early analysis about a company. He also waits patiently until the information becomes known and relevant to the Street. Until the Street knows what he knows, the information is theoretical. But eventually, for it to be of value to him as a trader, to give him a real edge, others must know it and act upon it as well. The information or differentiated view must become apparent to the market. The information he has must have reached the Street and changed the way other traders view that particular stock. The information is relevant only if others start selling a stock soon after he has shorted it. Therefore, when assessing a short, the short seller needs to ask himself three important questions:

1. Is my assessment objective or emotional?
2. What do I know that no one else knows?
3. When will the world accept my differentiated view?

Sometimes, the best shorts are put on in anticipation of a change in perception. While the fundamentals change very little, the anticipation of such a change in the fundamentals drives a stock. For example, those Old Economy companies that traders perceived to be vulnerable to Internet competition saw their stock prices pressured as traders anticipated an environment that would make business for them more difficult and less profitable. Often with New Economy concept stocks, perception of the company's future business prospects is all a trader has to go on. If not for changes in investor sentiments, how could one explain the large swings in many Internet stocks? Trading rationales such as "sell the news" or "it is reflected in the price of the stock" are often the basis for many short sales.

Although understanding the fundamental issues of a company are important, fundamentals alone are not enough to produce a successful short. In fact, shorting is especially difficult in a bear market because the fundamentals count for less in this kind of market. The trader then must rely on other resources and remain flexible in order to succeed at it. Indeed, much of this book is about the diverse skills a trader needs to enable him to succeed at more advanced strategies like shorting and taking advantage of capitulation.

Listen as Ralph, who specializes in trading competitive local exchange phone carriers, described how his stocks went down for macro or market reasons, not because of any bad news about the stocks.

"It is harder for me to short because these companies are growing," he said. "They go down dramatically. On the short side, I have problems with the timing. They rally, and then they drop. If you weren't there for that, then you won't make money. I don't have confidence in shorting these stocks because when they rally, they rally explosively. It used to be that I only shorted stocks because I had a good reason. Now in the last three weeks of May 2000, I can short any stock if it is expensive, regardless of the quality of the stock. I could short the best names if they were expensive. That is the mind-set change I had to make in the last three weeks. The market changes the rules in a day when you have been following the same rules for the past five years. The short-term model requires discipline. You have to cut your losses very quickly and control your risk."

When you are trading in the zone you can review all these factors and put the mosaic together including relevance and timing. To be successful at selling short, you have to understand the timeliness of information in terms of when it is available. Making sure the analysis is critical and timely is more important for shorts than for longs because the market is naturally biased toward the upside. You have to determine when the analysis will affect the stock price because others aren't responding yet. There are thousands of companies with questionable balance sheets and questionable practices. The market has to accept that information for it to be significant.

It is important not to be too anxious and thus too early. Often short sellers face adverse conditions or "pain" when making decisions on entries and exits. Trading in the zone and staying focused, disciplined, and unemotional makes it possible to minimize the pain.

Case Study

Al shorted a large brokerage firm when it was spinning out its online brokerage. He shorted it, and the stock gapped up. Sandy saw it. The stock then went from 78 to 85, to 90 then to 105. On the third day, Sandy shorted it at 105, 100, 102, 95. "He shorted a boatload," said Al. The next day the stock went down, and he started covering in the 86 to 94 range. But Al didn't.

"I was incapacitated by the fact that my positioning was wrong," he said. "I sat through a lot of pain and was unable to move. My position was too big. I couldn't maximize the position at the best possible time. You can be correct fundamentally, but if the timing is not correct because of the long bias in the market, you still lose.

In another trade, however, Al proved more wise.

"For a couple of months this HMO [health maintenance organization] was strong," Al said. "It seemed like it would go up forever. I quickly lost 20 points and immediately questioned the facts, both anecdotal and hard, that I had used to construct my case. For three years the shorts had been fighting to no avail. I figured I just was one more who was right, but wrong. After all, the idea is to make money! Fortunately, I stuck with it. Everyday, I called the local university hospital to confirm that the HMO owed $250 million. The numbers deteriorated as the claims payable as a percent of reserves soared. Insiders sold stock, lots of stock. In fact, the much-heralded CEO stepped down and sold his stock. Meanwhile, the sell-side kept pushing. All this information needed a focal point to bring it out."

"Why was this time different? What was my angle? The insurance commissioner was coming for a triannual audit. If the funda-

mentals were lousy, the commissioner would have to do something. Sure enough the commissioner called for a reinstatement,
and the stock plunged. It felt great to be vindicated, to be right in
the face of all the bullish and sloppy investors who ignored the
fundamentals. Interestingly enough all these issues were valid
three years prior but needed a catalyst. That is why a trader must
keep information in context. It's one thing to say something is rotten. It's another to say it when people are ready to embrace that it
is rotten."

Trading in the zone lets you stay calm and do the necessary work
to understand the companies you are shorting. It gives you the ability
to differentiate between what is illusion and reality, when fundamentals
do or don't matter. It even helps you to know when to play the illusion
and when to fade the illusion.

Managing the Psychology

A short squeeze occurs when buyers force the price of a stock upward
beyond the typical trading range. Those who have been shorting the
stock (selling it in the expectation that it will go down) begin to experience psychological pain that they will lose money and will be forced to
buy the stock back (cover it). As the price moves up, the shorts are
squeezed out of the stock. To cut their losses, shorts are forced to buy
it back at a higher price. At some point there may not be enough stock
available to be bought back, and the shorts are squeezed even more. At
that point, they are willing to pay whatever they have to buy the stock
back. This situation is known as a capitulation on the upside, which we
discussed in Chapter 12. This kind of situation—whether it leads to a
full capitulation or not—can be very emotionally disturbing. Learning
to manage the psychology behind the short squeeze is crucial to becoming a successful short seller.

Case Study
October 28, 1999, was a day the market turned upward, and the
shorts got squeezed. Al was one of those stuck in his shorts who
failed to cover. He was short two large cap stocks.

"I am tired," said Al. "I want to take stuff down. I am stuck. I am not enjoying the pain. It went up five points. Instead of covering, I said, 'The hell with it.' It went up another 10, then 15. I thought I was right, but I didn't have a strong reason for it. I wasn't paying attention to what was going on around me. I lost it and hoped to get it back. I made $500,000 one day. I lost $450,000 the next day. Instead of doing something proactively, I figured I would get it back the next day. I am moving off my game. I feel exhausted and can't think through things. I feel isolated."

Many traders often get emotionally carried away on the short side. Sometimes they are unable to admit they are wrong early and become frozen, "wishing" for the stock to come down. The move itself generates strong emotions, and traders have to learn to be able to hold their positions when appropriate and to cover their short positions to cut their losses when the stock is too strong or their original reasons for shorting are no longer correct.

Trading in the zone enables you to stay relaxed and able to buy when there is weakness and sell when there is strength. When a stock is running up, everyone keeps buying because they think it is going higher. That is what creates reversals. Trading in the zone will give you the confidence to start shorting a stock when you see that. You won't feel squeezed in. You will be able to short more as the stock continues to rally against you, in order to bring your cost basis up in order to help make more money.

"I have had situations where the price action didn't confirm what I knew, and I got scared out of my fundamental position and didn't take the big positions. If you have a strong conviction about the fundamentals and can see the case emerging, that provides support," said Al. "When negative news comes out, and a stock stops going down or even goes up, you have to question if you have reached an inflection point. Ironically, most people wait for a confirming view of the stock price, and when it moves they do not want to pay up for it since they failed to get in earlier based on their fundamental assessment. To be a great trader, I have to come up with a verifiable and dynamic thesis. But if something radical happens which challenges my view, I have to make my bet or recognize that things have changed and get out.

For example, 10 years ago one big insurance company was thought to be a joke. Continual allegations of insurance fraud and accounting issues dogged the stock. The stock had a terrific run, going up thousands of percent, but after 10 years, it collapsed. Though ultimately right, traders who shorted the stock throughout the years, thinking the fundamentals were bogus, lost money."

For most people the emotional aspects of a short can paralyze. They hold on when it is not working and hope that the next tick will be the last higher tick and the stock will soon fall. If you are trading in the zone you can watch the price of your short move up and buy the stock back and keep your losses down. Remember, most people think it must be a good company if the price is going up, but that's not always true. That is why it is incumbent on the short seller to understand the business model—which ones work and don't work.

Case Study
Listen as one trader described the difficulty of this process. On Wednesday, September 9, 1999, traders were being short squeezed again. The shorts were finding fewer ideas. Their positions were being threatened as the market rebounded. The shorts were starting to panic as prices moved upward. Rollie wondered if he could take the pain or whether he should cover his shorts and lose one million dollars.

"On Thursday I wanted to cover this stuff. I didn't, and I blew $300,000 on Friday," he explained. "I am short all these market surrogates. My losses are a distraction to me. I was nervous because I was doing well. I had a foreboding that it was going to end. I don't have a game plan or a sense of clarity on my stories. I don't have names. Everything is up, and I can't see why it is going to go down near term. It will go down two weeks from now, but should I sit here and lose money in the meantime? Granted the fundamentals are in trouble, but why do I want to be in one of the ten stocks that the world is gravitating to?"

There is a psychological tendency to want to buy the bottom and short the top. That mentality can be troublesome to the short seller. You have to be skeptical but not cynical. You also have to be objective. If you are not objective, then you become emotional and are trying too hard to "get it right." From a money management viewpoint that can be deadly.

The psychological aspect of short selling is one of the most difficult aspects of this type of trading. It is not being a contrarian. You shouldn't short simply to short. You have to have a reason and create a thesis—a train of thought from which to trade.

As discussed throughout this book, the overwhelming fear and panic that a trader faces in the possibility of loss can cause him to trade based on his emotions instead of his intellect. Shorting stocks because you believe they are going down requires some degree of equanimity, particularly when a lot of people have shorted a stock and there is little stock left for borrowing. How well you handle a short squeeze depends on your ability to maintain your composure in the face of pain. The best traders can tolerate the price rises and get out when the price actions show that they are wrong.

"It is great to be right intellectually, and it is frustrating to see things I've honed in on go the other way," said Al. "I have to remember to react to the price action and the money flows and not hold on so tightly to my thesis, no matter how right it may *eventually* prove to be."

Trading in the zone helps you develop the ability not to overrationalize the short when it is going up and against you and not to justify staying in to make more money when it comes down. The master trader knows when to get out of the short by covering and taking a loss and can determine when to press the bet.

Shorting is another weapon in the trader's arsenal. It is especially relevant to those who want to run a balanced portfolio, capitalizing on the ups and downs in the market. But it is also a strategy that works best for those who are able to stay centered and trade in the zone.

Conclusion

Since *Trading to Win* was published in 1998, I have been asked repeatedly about the basic principles involved in helping traders to maximize their performances and profitability. The answer to this question is complex, but the one thing that stands out above all else is the willingness to commit to specific results and then to do all the work necessary to realize those results. This is easier said than done, since most traders, like most people, have a difficult time grasping the concept of commitment—the concept that they can create the world by promising the future and then living in terms of their promise.

However, this type of commitment is not merely a matter of words. Commitment to your results is an existential act of courage that will enable you to get over your fears, self-doubts, and anxiety so as to maximize your achievements way beyond anything you ever thought possible before. It is a process of self-examination and self-monitoring. It demands that you scrutinize your own behavior and attitudes, which may be keeping you from trading in the zone.

My work is focused on maximizing performance as well as helping traders recover their nerve and confidence after large drawdowns. Thus, I encourage all traders:

- To adhere to their strategy and discipline and most of all to get out of losers and add to winners within the framework of achieving daily targets.

- To set reasonable objectives—maintain or regain confidence by making predictable amounts each day. If a trader is recovering from big losses, I encourage him to start with smaller numbers.

- To look at each position on its own merits and not justify being in a losing stock because of gains in another one.

- To establish rules about closing down trading after big losses and not trying to retrieve past losses. The key is not trying to make money back, but to trade to win every time. Keep losses small. Push winning trades.

- To stop fighting the tape and to measure the risk/reward of each position and to continuously reevaluate the risk/reward as the trade moves. It is that constant reevaluation that allows you to trade well.

If you want to trade in the zone, you have to be willing to consider what you must change about yourself by asking tough questions, such as "What are you doing now that you don't want to do?" and "What is it that you know you must do but are afraid to do?" Consider, for example:

- How much energy do you expend on tasks that you are doing out of a sense of habit or obligation or to meet the expectations of others?

- How much are you rationalizing your trading losses?

- How much do you fail to take advantage of opportunities without looking closely at what bits of your behavior you might change?

- What are the steps you know you must take but which you are putting off because of inertia, laziness, or self-doubt?

A specific financial goal or target for the day, the week, or the month will fortify you against the distractions that come from judging yourself in terms of standards of the past and the expectations of others. It will help you to stop fixating on negative experiences or reasons for failure and get you thinking more positively about the incremental steps you can take to accomplish the tasks at hand. A trading goal will give you a standard against which to make decisions about activities to avoid and make it easier to assume responsibility for actions to take that will help you to master fear and anxiety and step into the abyss of possibility.

If most of what you have accomplished until now resulted from using only a portion of your abilities, think how much more satisfying things will be once you begin to use all of your talents in pursuit of a goal and spend less energy in masking your anxieties and in maintaining certain kinds of defensive postures. A goal or vision of future results creates a context of possibility, very much as a canvas provides the artist with a context in which to paint. The canvas shapes the magnitude and parameters of the painting and sets the boundaries. You select a goal and then, within the frame of the goal, fill in what's missing. The goal draws you to action and creates the moment-by-moment experience of your trades. Put another way, you set up a goal and then reverse-engineer all the steps you must begin to take to realize that goal.

You can reach any goal you commit yourself to reaching, not by magical or positive thinking, but through action—by trading in ways that are consistent with your goal rather than functioning automatically in terms of a limiting, self-protective notion of yourself. Commitment to the goal is not some arbitrary concept but rather a powerful beacon that empowers you to act decisively in the face of internal thoughts of "I can't" do it or "shouldn't" do it. Commitment to a goal means promising the result and following a trading strategy in line with that result.

The purpose of a goal is to give you a direction for focusing. By developing a strategy consistent with your goal, you will be able to overcome any inclination for indecision and procrastination. Following your strategy will give you a sense of direction and excitement.

Perform the steps that are necessary to reach your target each day. As you succeed, raise the stakes. Be willing to do things that are not ordinarily part of your repertoire, behaving in ways that do not seem "like you." Be willing to find out what is missing, seek more information, and ask for help and support. Expand or enlarge your goal to increase the level of the challenge and bring more of your hidden potential into play.

You cannot assume things will be taken care of. You must produce the results. You must be clear with those who are assisting you about what you want and must review your plans with them. Don't assume things will go the way you want them to go unless you outline your regimens and establish a structure to ensure the outcome.

Keep visualizing the results and taking action consistent with the results, noticing where you stop and what gets in the way of your committed action. Slowly but surely, this visual imagery rehearsal will help you to create what is missing so that you bring reality into alignment with your vision. When you move beyond your fears and concerns, you will generate breakthroughs beyond what you believed possible.

But remember, you may also experience a sense of losing control because it doesn't seem as if you are able to control the results. In fact, this sense of losing control often occurs when your life stops being predictable and starts happening in line with the new actions that you are taking.

So, don't postpone your actions because of uncomfortable feelings that may arise as a result of them. The longer you wait to act, the more likely you are to create problems and obstacles in your mind, which will lead to more delay and a greater tendency to be governed by preconceptions.

If you put most of your energy into planning and preparation rather than actually engaging in the tasks at hand, you will not reach your target. In fact, you will tend more often to remain in place and keep doing more of what you have already been doing. You may get good at preparation and planning but will not develop the kind of knowledge that comes only from engaging in the activity itself.

To learn white water rafting, it is necessary to ride the rapids. You may want to read a book on white water rafting before you do it. You may want to talk to some friends who have experience in this activity. You may even need assistance from a guide. But you won't actually learn how to white water raft until you do it. It is only when you actually go white water rafting that you experience the unpredictability and risk of the ride. It is only by being in the raft, on the rapids, that you will truly learn the importance of following the rules. There is a level of information that only can be derived from the experience itself. Moreover, there are always events that cannot be predicted and that you can only discover by participating in the experience.

The value of action is that it enables you to see an aspect of reality quite distinct from your concepts of reality. Action breaks through your fixed way of seeing things and enables you to see the truth between the cracks, before ideas about the event are fixed and become part of a concept about the experience.

What you need to discover about trading, you can only gain from participation in the event itself. Your trading success is dependent on your response to the events themselves, not from your thoughts or interpretations about them.

Essentially, you need action to see beneath the veneer or the facade of reality. This is what the Japanese mean by *satori*—a space in the world that you can't see until you take action consistent with your vision. So, don't wait for perfection or certainty, and don't be burdened by details, self-doubt, or the need to look good.

Remember, living the vision does not occur simply because you verbally commit to it, nor will it be a matter of mere effort. To live your vision requires a radical decision to produce specific results consistent with the target and then to take on the result like your life depended on it. If you keep going and keep risking yourself by getting past your discomforting thoughts, you have the possibility to enter into a realm of being where the moment before you becomes intense and extraordinary. If you can stay with these feelings and bodily sensations you will soon reach the zone.

While commitment to your vision means to do all that is necessary to produce it, at the same time you should not become overly attached to the result so that you are distressed when you don't produce it or are overegotistical when you do. While you may feel excited and fulfilled by achieving a goal, and while this may enhance your confidence and self-esteem, winning should not be an end in itself.

Your goal is a directional device and a source of inspiration or motivation. You play to win, but the game is not about winning. Success does not actually come when you reach your target. It comes from playing the game wholeheartedly, tapping all of your energies and potential. There are no shortcuts or easy results. Commitment is about being fully engaged in your trades, not about reaching the goal. Even when you reach your target, you must be careful not to become enthralled with yourself or full of pride. For then you will surely lose it. Indeed, once you reach your goal you must create new and larger goals if you are to continue to stay in the zone.

Certain things will become apparent along the way. One basic principle that you will discover sooner or later is that you and you alone are responsible for making your career work. What happens for you is based on your willingness to take responsibility for your trades. Once you accept responsibility for what happens, and don't simply blame the markets or even yourself (which too diverts attention away from the tasks at hand), you can start making decisions about the direction in which you want things to go. Then you will soon have greater influence over the outcome of your trades.

This simple change of perspective to trade in the realm of action, purpose, and self-determination will have an enormous effect on the way you experience your trading and even your life. When you see how your own perspective influences events and you consciously accept responsibility for what happens in your trading, you no longer feel like the hapless victim of circumstances at the mercy of forces that are beyond your control.

Don't focus on the drift or the natural inclination to make interpretations of why things aren't going the way you want them to go. Don't rush. Don't push too hard. It is not a matter of effort or trying harder or doing more of whatever you have been doing. It is just a matter of focused attention on producing concrete results related to your target.

As you focus you start to see how much your self-doubt and uncertainty are kept alive by your need to hide your weakness and to appear stronger than you are. If you can acknowledge your failings and declare breakdowns when they exist, you can create the structure of support that you need to produce results consistent with your vision and independent of the habits that now dominate your life.

As you move toward your goals, keep processing information about how things are going, without judging yourself or succumbing to the criticism of the inner voices or perpetual conversation that too often runs your life. Keep listening for the support of the people around whenever you can acknowledge their contribution to your efforts.

It is also essential to establish the trust of others because doing so ensures that they understand what it is that you want them to do, even if the people helping you are experts at what they do. Establish a systematic way of checking on what is done so that you can be certain people are participating in accord with your plan. Establish a system of checks and balances so that you can periodically review their efforts. Correct the tasks and realign the targets to make certain that what you want accomplished will in fact be done. You have to specify what you want; otherwise you can anticipate failure.

It is important to recognize that the early stages of a project usually involve more effort and fewer results. Be willing to put the initial effort in without seeing too many results, with the knowledge that down the line there will be greater results. This is a matter of faith. Too many people give up in the early stages when they don't see results, without realizing that it takes considerable effort to create the structure necessary for ensuring positive outcomes.

Taking responsibility for your trading results means being willing to stand in the gap between where you are and where you are going. You must be able to respond to reality as it is from your true self without trying to change yourself or the people around you or your circumstances. It is not a matter of willpower but a matter of acting in the world consistent with your vision and not in terms of your preconceptions. When you relinquish your perfectionism and accept your vulnerability and humanity, you will stop trying to force things and will be able to allow events to unfold in line with your vision. Then you will begin to see possibilities in the marketplace you couldn't see before.

Obviously by reading this book you are taking a stand that you wish to improve your approach to trading. You are seeking to free yourself from the bondage of fears and habits that may have limited your trading potential. It is the willingness to trade today in a new way consistent with producing the results you have chosen to realize, irrespective of whether there is any evidence or certainty about this. It is the willingness to take responsibility for the way your trading unfolds from this moment on, trading in the gap in an unpremeditated way.

This means you have to accept anxiety and fear as part of trading at the level of commitment to a stretch target.

The market is what it is, even though it may not be what you expect it to be. If you don't try to change things but accept things as they are, you will experience the world in an entirely new way. As Rainer Marie Rilke said: "The future enters into us in order to transform itself in us, long before it happens."

There is a reality in the world that you cannot perceive because you are limited by what you believe you know. If you can let go of your preconceptions and life principles long enough to see what is in the world in terms of a larger creative vision, you will begin to see new opportunities for trading in a powerful and stimulating way.

You have the power to change by committing to a larger vision and letting go of your automatic self-protective notions. By creating a new vision and acting consistently with the vision, you transform the realm of your being and behaving. You tap into the hidden potential within yourself and the universe where you can live beyond the limits of ego, anxiety, and habit.

The goal is a place from which to come. It is a statement about how things ought to be that gives you a place from which to trade. It is a stand to take, a way of trading defined by the result. When you commit to your goal and begin to trade consistently with your strategy, you will see what's missing from your trading. You will learn the fundamentals, minimize your risk versus your return, gain knowledge, and take all the other steps explored within this book to see what needs to be discovered or developed in order to reach your target. When you take this action, when you trade in terms of a consistent plan to reach a specified target, you commit your full self to the task at hand, and then you will finally experience the exhilarating power of trading in the zone.

Index

active passivity, 175–176
adaptability, 171–172
adjustment, inability for, 170–174
advanced strategies
    capitulation, 195–204
    short selling, 205–218
analysts, 66, 84–86
anxiety
    dealing with, 3, 7–8, 24, 42, 45–47, 119, 138, 226
    paralysis and, 165
    physiological components of, record of, 121, 168
    sources of, 121, 125
averaging down, 142–144, 172–173

balanced portfolio, 15, 112–115
balance sheet, 60, 65, 84
behavior modification, 28–32
    risk management and, 104–108
belief system, 12, 22, 93, 174
benchmarks, 92, 207
bonds, 77–79, 191
bond traders, 191
boredom, 183, 187–188
bottoms, picking, 136–138
burnout, 169, 187–188

capital allocation, risk management and, 101–104
capitulation
    collapsing market, trading in, 199–201
    defined, 196–199
    inflection, 201–204
catalysts
    identification of, 148, 151
    impact of, generally, 80, 87–88, 104, 139, 152
challenges
    burnout and, 187–188
    focus and, 183–185
    importance of, 176–178, 190
    objectives and, 190–191
    opinions, 186–187
    stopping points, identification of, 180–183

visual imagery rehearsals, 178–180
    withdrawal and, 188–190
commitment
    importance of, 7, 13, 20, 34, 48–49, 219, 221, 223–224
    prioritizing, 40
competition, awareness of, 88, 92
complacency, 169–170, 182
confidence
    importance of, 2, 15, 18–20, 48–49, 60, 164, 179, 188
    risk management and, 109–111
    sources of, 82, 126, 129
consistent trading
    challenges, 175–191
    mistakes, learning from, 135–155
    psychological obstacles, overcoming, 157–174
contrarian investing, 29, 64, 138, 212
conviction
    importance of, 16, 47, 130
    mistakes and, 142, 146
countertrend signals, 60
cyclical stocks, 15–16, 66

day traders, 65, 149
decision-making
    emotional responses, 122, 144–145, 147
    influences on, 6, 82, 87–92
defensive behavior, 3, 26, 186, 200
denial, 31
depression, 123–125, 175
discipline, importance of, 18, 45, 138, 170, 191, 204, 213–214, 219
drawdowns, 129–130, 143
drivers, identification of, 56, 63

earnings
    implications of, 83–84, 87, 95, 104, 115
    missed, 210–211
economic indicators, 73–74
ego, 149, 179, 186
emotional response
    impact of, 3, 7–8, 30, 42, 93–94, 118
    mistakes due to, 144–145

emotional response, *continued*
  negative, 175
  short selling and, 215–218
emotions
  control of, 121–125
  importance of controlling, 118–120, 137, 139, 202
  tracking emotions, 168
entry points, 6, 45, 173
equity traders, 75, 115, 191
exit points, 6, 100, 191

failure, fear of, 3, 6, 24, 26
fear
  cycle of, 28–29
  dealing with, 3, 6–7, 16, 18, 121–122, 175
  decision-making and, 122
  as motivation, 80
  overcoming, 112, 225–226
  risk management and, 106, 112
  in risk-taking, 162
  short selling and, 218
flexibility, importance of, 125, 170, 172
focus. *See also* goal-setting strategies
  challenges and, 183–185
  importance of, 16–17, 20, 126, 197, 214
  information gathering and, 82, 86
  long-term, 7
  losing positions and, 139
  risk management and, 131
fundamentals
  analysis of, 31
  decision-making and, 87–92
  reevaluation of, 82
  short selling and, 212–215

gambling, 5, 26, 103
goals
  challenging, 110–111
  daily, 37–38, 129, 173, 220
  importance of, 33–34, 40, 143, 181, 220–221, 226
  review of, 35
  setting, *see* goal-setting strategies
goal-setting strategies
  commitment and, 34, 48–49
  impact of, 34–38
  implementation of, 41–45
  importance of, 48
  mindset, maintaining, 45–46
  performance, rationalizing, 47–48
  reactions, restructuring, 47
  resistance to, 38–40
greed, 80, 139, 142, 204

habits, 22, 174, 189, 225
herding, 31–32, 81, 199

holding periods, 14, 101, 106–107, 141, 145–147

imagery, 178–180
implementation, goal-setting strategies
  past trades, examination of, 41–43
  results, review of, 43–45
inflection points, 201–204, 207
information gathering
  analysis, 54–56, 173
  decision-making and, 87–92
  importance of, 53–54, 82–83
  information processing, 60–65, 174
  pertinent information, determination of, 56–59
  timing, 65–68
  unseen variables, 92–95
  valuation, 83–87
information management, 58–59
insecurity, *see* fear
instincts
  confirmation of, 57
  trust in, 17, 46, 130
interest rates, 62, 78–79
Internet stocks, 63, 186, 201
interpretive skills, 56–59
intraday volatility, 15, 82, 112, 114–115
intuition, 76, 148–149
investment style, 152–153
IPOs (initial public offerings), 89, 197

knowledge, importance of, 14, 40. *See also* information gathering

limitations, identification of, 22–27
liquidity, 79, 128, 139
listening skills, 60–61
long positions, fundamentals and, 89–90
losing positions, 6, 108, 114, 138–144
losing trades, 37, 106, 126–127
loss aversion, 28–30
losses. *See also* losing trades
  average, 102
  repeated, 48, 126
  succession of, 168, 189–190
  winning back, 7, 220

macroeconomics
  applications of, 74–77, 79–80
  short selling and, 207
market rallies, 14, 61–62, 72
market timing, 46, 65–68
market volatility, 3, 15, 82, 109, 128, 153
master traders, strategies of, 56–57, 59–60, 85, 90, 92, 94–95, 100, 109, 111, 126, 128, 136–137, 148, 154, 162, 170–171, 190–191, 199–200, 202–204

maximizing trading, 29–30
mindset
    focused, 49
    impact of, generally, 3–4
    maintaining, 45–46
    negative, 46, 126, 130, 167, 175
    positive, 161, 177–178
mistakes
    averaging down, 142–144, 172–173
    bidding for stocks, 147–148
    failing to take profits, 144–147
    holding onto losers, 138–144
    intuition, relying on, 148–149
    learning from, 27–28, 54–55, 114,
        135–136, 161
    loyalty, 140
    missed opportunities, 141
    overtrading, 149–150
    "Poor Me" syndrome, 166–168
    reviewing, 150–155
    saving face, 140–142
    Seller's Remorse, 159–161
    stub ends, 142
    tops and bottoms, picking, 136–138
momentum
    determination of, 80
    psychological, 7, 43
motivation
    challenges and, 183
    loss of, 34

negative trades, 44, 119–120
news, impact of, 87–88

objectives. *See also* goal(s); goal-setting
        strategies
    challenges and, 190–191
    creation of, 176, 220
objectivity, 171, 208
opinions, 186–187
overanalyzing, 161–163
overtrading, 103, 123, 125, 149–150
overvalued stock, 207, 209

pain, dealing with, 175, 214
panic, dealing with, 123–125, 199, 201, 218
paralysis, 161–165, 190
passivity, 158
past programming
    goal-setting and, 36
    identifying, 22–27
perfectionism, 29, 107, 161–165
performance, rationalizing, 47–48, 220
perspectives, implications of, 12, 58, 93, 224
"Poor Me" syndrome, 166–168
portfolio
    assessment of, 15

balanced, 15, 112–115
    volatility of, 105, 109–10
position
    assessment of, 122–123
    size of, 37–38, 45, 47, 146
preparation
    analysis, 69–80, 173
    importance of, 202, 222
    information gathering, 53–68, 174
    research, 81–95
price movement, 71–72
pride, dealing with, 122–123
prioritizing, 40, 185
procrastination, 165
profitability, 7, 16, 100, 102, 104, 109, 143
profit and loss (P&L), 13, 19, 30, 101–102,
        188
profit-taking, 144–147
psychological obstacles, overcoming
    adjustment, inability for, 170–174
    complacency, 169–170
    importance of, 157–159, 174
    paralysis, 161–165
    passivity, 158
    perfectionism, 161–165
    "Poor Me" syndrome, 166–168
    Seller's Remorse, 159–161
psychology of trading
    implications of, 3, 6, 81, 123
    short selling, 215–218

rationalization, 45, 47–48, 143, 146, 184, 220
reactions, restructuring, 47
reframing, 7, 46, 145
regret, 161. *See also* Seller's Remorse
rejection, 30–31
remorse, *see* Seller's Remorse
resistance, dealing with, 3, 16, 38–40, 154
risk averse traders, 157
risk management
    balanced portfolio and, 112–115
    importance of, 99–101
    size of position, 108–112
    statistics, review of, 101–108
risk managers, reviewing statistics and,
        102–103
risk profile, 18
risk/reward ratio, 63, 108, 220
risk-taking, 2, 39, 162
risk tolerance
    assessment of, 99, 117
    emotions, control of, 118–125, 137, 139
    losses, handling strategies, 126–131
rumors, response to, 68, 87, 141

saving face, 140–142
scalping, 103, 110

self, sense of, 111
self-awareness, importance of, 26
self-blame, 166
self-characterizations, 3
self-confidence, 191
self-control, 35
self-criticism, 18
self-destructive behavior, 35
self-determination, 224
self-fulfilling prophecies, 3, 19
self-justification, 31
self-protection, 226
self-reliance, 188
self-sabotage, 46, 190
Seller's Remorse, 159–161
Sharpe ratio, 37
short selling
    defined, 205
    good short, components of, 208–212
    missed earnings, 210–211
    mistakes in, 136, 141–142
    on positives, 211–212
    psychology of, 215–218
    thesis development and, 206–208
    timing and relevance, 212–215
short-term trading, 66
signposts, awareness of, 64
site visits, 86–87
size of position, 37–38, 45, 47, 108–112, 131, 146
Small T personality, 157
spreadsheets, 144, 153–154
statistics, review of, 101–108
stopping points, identification of, 180–183
stress
    dealing with, 18
    reduction strategies, 106
stub ends, 142
success factors, generally, 100, 112, 114, 222–223
successful trades
    repeated, 175
    timing and, 67–68
supply and demand, 62, 81, 123

target(s)
    achievement of, 40
    daily, 82, 139, 161, 219–220
    increasing, 20
    losing trades and, 128
    risk management and, 105
    stretch, 189, 226
    succession of, 43

technical analysis
    applications of, generally, 70–71
    bonds, 77–79
    indicators, 71–74
    interpretation and, 79–80
    macroeconomic variables, 75–77
technical indicators, 71–74
    understanding of, 82
technology stocks, 44, 63, 88, 186–187
thesis
    changes to, 152
    development of, 57, 62, 65, 206–208
    focus on, 163
    importance of, 154
time horizon, 82, 191
tops, picking, 136–138
track record, reestablishment of, 173
trades, number of, 149, 163–164
trading coach, function of, 180
trading objectives, 13
trading style, 4, 104, 172
Trading to Win, 1–2, 4, 135, 164, 195–196, 219
trends, interpretation of, 60–61
trust
    development of, 225
    in instincts, 17, 46, 130
200-day moving average, 72–73
Type T personality, 157

uncertainty, 7, 40, 28, 121, 124, 138, 191

valuation, 62, 80, 83–87, 94
vision
    alignment with, 190
    clarity of, 46
    commitment to, 223, 225–226
    importance of, 13, 25, 222–223
    obstacles to, 24–25
visual imagery rehearsals, 178–180

win/loss ratio, 108
winning trades, 6, 37, 101, 106–107
wins, rejecting of, 30–31
withdrawal, 188–190
wu-wei, 175–176

Zone, generally
    characteristics of, 16–18
    defined, 2, 11–13
    entering, 14–16
    staying in, 12–13, 18–20